73- 78 5 Islamic Pillars

MW01268159

What Every Christian Should Know About Islam

by

Christian S. Anderson

Copyright © 2008 by Christian S. Anderson

What Every Christian Should Know About Islam
by Christian S. Anderson

Printed in the United States of America

ISBN 978-1-60647-442-6

All rights reserved solely by the author. The author guarantees all contents are original and do not infringe upon the legal rights of any other person or work. No part of this book may be reproduced in any form without the permission of the author. The views expressed in this book are not necessarily those of the publisher.

Unless otherwise indicated, Bible quotations are taken from The King James Version of the Bible. Copyright © 1976 by Thomas Nelson, Inc., Publishers.

All verses from the Quran are quoted from Muhammad Marmaduke Pickthall's *The Glorious Qur'an*, Muslim World League, Grand Central Station, New York City, NY, 1977.

www.xulonpress.com

Forward

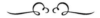

As one looks at the direction of the world today it doesn't take a college education to see there is battle going on for the hearts and minds of people. There are many religions, but few have arisen with such fervor as Islam. Because of its spread across many nations of the world, it is imperative to have at least a cursory knowledge of both the historical background and the doctrinal tenants of this religion.

This book is written by a Christian for Christians who are interested in knowing more about Islam. Most Christians see other religions through their own frame of reference. We come to faith through a personal choice after hearing the good news that Jesus Christ died on the cross paying the price for our sins and restoring to us the ability to have a personal relationship with God.

Yet personal choice is not how most Muslims come to faith or stay in their faith. Proof of this can be seen today in many places of the world, but none more blatant and under-reported than in Sudan, where Muslim forces are exterminating the non-Muslim (mostly Christian) population who refuse to convert to Islam. Another proof is seen in the duty of Muslim fathers to kill family members who choose another religion over Islam. Muslims who choose to convert must stay secretive or else become martyrs.

A truthful look at modern-day history shows us the dark side of Islam. Since Israel became a nation again, many Arab clerics and political leaders have embraced a philosophy of annihilation towards both Jews and Christians. Frequently, we see reports in the media of continual warring by Islamic fanatics towards others, including those with a different view of Islam. Jihad is a word most westerners associate with holy war against us. Yet these issues are dismissed when Islam is presented as a religion of peace.

As Christians trying to understand Islam, we find there is much information about Islam offering conflicting theological views, historical inaccuracies, and obvious biases attempting to portray Islam in a more favorable light than historical data actually would permit. To be fair, the same has happened with Christianity. It is historically factual that genocidal atrocities were carried out by those claiming to be true to the name of Jesus Christ. However, unlike the Quran, the Bible nowhere advocates violence as an instrument of evangelism.

Though many have tried to discredit Christianity, the basic claims of biblical Christianity have been shown to be historically accurate, archaeologically true, and even scientifically verified in many cases. The text of the Bible has a very high degree of accuracy in transmission through the centuries. Likewise, the corpus of Christian theology has been through the refining fire.

The time has come for Islamic history and theology to come under the microscope. If the claims of Muhammed are true, they should be historically verifiable and accurate. If the theology of Muhammed is of God, then it should remain constant and not change to become more palatable and marketable to the masses. If Islam is as some claim it is, then Islam should at least be able to withstand the same basic critical methods as have been applied to biblical Christianity. Simply put, how does the foundation of Islam stand under examination of basic historical, archaeological and theological methods of criticism? This book addresses these concerns.

In writing this forward, let me also introduce you to the author, Christian Anderson. Chris has faithfully attended and taught in the church that I pastored for over 15 years. He is a humble intellectual with a brilliant mind. He knows the biblical languages and grammatical-historical methodology. He came to author this work out of love and concern for those who have little understanding of the facts behind the religion of Islam. His writing of this work was initiated by the leading of the Holy Spirit, a decision he agonized over for months. I should also say that Chris spent many years researching the facts used in writing this book.

One final address to Christians and friends of Israel: this book is a wakeup call to pray. Though many today claim Islam is peaceful, history shows the opposite. The war was declared long ago. Dark and sinister forces are at work behind the religion of Islam. Their goal is total subjugation and slavery of mankind. Let us pray for the truth about Islam to come to light. Let us also pray for the people who follow Muhammed to have a revelation of the Prince of Peace, the Lord Jesus Christ. Also let us pray that the true God will, once again intervene in the affairs of mankind and bring His judgment upon the dark spiritual forces at work vying for the hearts of mankind.

Tom Comstock
Senior Pastor
Blue Mountain Christian Center
Grand Terrace, California

Table of Contents

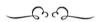

Chapter 1: Historical Antecedents to Islam

Introduction

Muslims look at the many Bible versions and denominations of Christianity and falsely conclude it surely could not have been properly thought through (see Hansen, p. 112). They see both Judaism and Christianity as stillborn attempts by Allah to bring Islam to mankind, which were corrupted by unfaithful followers. It is a Muslim dogma that the tenants of Islam came to Muhammed directly from Allah Himself. It is believed by Muslims that their holy book, called the Quran, is eternal. However, as this chapter will reveal, Islam has historical anteced-ents, as does any belief system. Christians have no problem with historical antecedents, since God has spoken to humanity in time and space. Thus, the Bible is interpreted using the grammatical/historical method, hence, the great importance of the homily and modern Bible translations in Christianity. The ancient languages and historical setting of the Bible have to be interpreted to be made relevant to the modern church-goer. It is obvious that Muhammed borrowed entirely from his native culture and older religious traditions in compiling the Islamic religion. These sources include: (1) Semitic and (2) Arab culture, (3) Pre-Islamic Paganism, (4) Christianity, (5) Judaism, and (6) Sabeanism.

I. The Semites

The term Semite, used in its modern sense, is a linguistic and not a racial term. Originally, it indicated descent from Shem, one of the sons of Noah. The Semitic group of languages has its origin on the African continent and is related to the Hamitic language group. Hamitic languages are no longer separated from the Semitic languages by modern linguists (Bohannan and Curtain, p. 42). Semitic, Hamitic, and Chadic languages are lumped together into what is called the Afro-Asiatic group (Hallet, p. 31).

The Semitic branch of the Afro-Asiatic language group is divided into *East Semitic* (Akkadian), *Northwest Semitic* (Ugaritic, Punic, Phoenician, Biblical Hebrew, Rabbinical Hebrew, Modern Hebrew, Aramaic, Syriac), and *Southwest Semitic* (Arabic, Ethiopic, Amharic).

Semitic-speaking peoples crossed the Bab el Mandeb into the Arabian Peninsula in pre-historic times. Over the centuries they migrated north oasis by oasis. Before 4000 B.C. these Semites had settled in

Syria and were moving into the plain of Shinar from there and south from the Arabian Desert (Newlon, p. 57). At about the same time a people of uncertain origin speaking an agglutinative language not clearly related to any other was settling the southern part of the region near the Persian Gulf. They developed a high civilization commonly known as Sumer. They built the cities of Nippur, Adab, Lagash, Umma, Larsa, Erech, Eridu, and Ur. The Semites established the following cities: Babylon, Borsippa, Dilbat, Kish, Kuthah, Opis, Sippar, and Agade (Accad). Akkad, the country north of Sumer, takes its name from the city of Agade. The East Semitic language Akkadian also comes from the name of this city.

There are a number of Semitic characteristics which are of great importance for understanding Islam. First of all, Semites were among the few ancient peoples who used a lunar calendar of 354 days. Such a calendar is still used in Islam for ceremonial purposes. The Hebrews also used a 354-day calendar but added an extra intercalary month (Veadar) seven times in every complete lunar cycle of 19 years in order to bring the lunar year into correspondence with the solar year.

Secondly, contrary to most ancient peoples, the Semites generally worshipped the moon-god as a male deity and the sun as a goddess. The planet Venus was significant, as well, and was worshipped as the goddess Ishtar.

The seven-day week is also a Semitic contrivance. Both the ancient Egyptians and Greeks divided the month into three ten-day periods. Originally, the

Romans had an eight-day week. The Semitic week is based on the phases of the moon.

The ancient Hebrews also used a seven-day week. However, the significance for them had nothing to do with the phases of the moon but was based, rather, on the seven days of creation (Gen. 1:3-2:3). This passage is a polemic against the gods of the heathen. The LORD GOD created earth, sky, oceans, and heavenly bodies, as well as plants, animals, and humans. For the heathen nations sweet and salt waters were themselves deities. Earth was the great Mother Goddess. The sun, moon, and stars were worshipped. According to heathen mythology, human beings were created to serve as attendants for these deities, i.e., to be their slaves (Frankfort, Wilson, and Jacobsen, pp. 148, 149).

Furthermore, we must consider the close connection between religion and nationality, which is another Semitic trait. The story of Ruth illustrates this. As a native of Moab, she would have been a devotee of the national god Chemosh. In order to reside with her mother-in-law Naomi in the land of Israel, Ruth would have to forsake her former religious identity and become a worshipper of Israel's God Yahweh. "Thy people shall be my people, and thy God my God," she declared (Ruth 1:16). This is still true today. A Muslim is an Arab first no matter what his country of origin. On the other hand, Middle Eastern Christians identify themselves by the country of their birth. Thus, Coptic Christians call themselves Egyptians and Marionite Christians say they are Lebanese. Lamsa explains:

"In the East, race and religion are inseparable. No one can be loyal to a race if he tries to weaken its faith and traditions. This is because the race is governed by the justice and morality derived from religion. Therefore, disloyalty to religion would be disloyalty to the race and the state" (p. 161).

The last Semitic characteristic we will consider is a legal principle. This principle is known as that of *lex talionis*—the law of retaliation. It is exemplified in the Mosaic Code as "an eye for an eye, a tooth for a tooth" (Ex. 21:24). The *lex talionis* is also the legal theory behind the code of King Hammurabi of Babylon (c.1792-1749 B.C.). This principle is greatly influential in *sharia*, the legal system that governs Islamic states (Spencer, p. 4).

II. Arabia and the Arabs

The Arabian Peninsula is a great plateau bounded on the south by the Indian Ocean, on the east by the Arabian Sea, on the north by the Persian Gulf, and on the west by the Red Sea. The peninsula is home to six nations—Saudi Arabia, Yemen, Oman, the United Arab Emirates, Qatar, and Kuwait. Additionally, the island nation of Bahrain lies in the Persian Gulf just off the Saudi and Qatari coasts. Bahrain is the ancient Dilmun of the Gilgamesh Epic.

In the Hebrew *arab* seems to mean "waste" or "desert" (cf. Ethiopic *abra*, "to be dry"). An ancient people known as the Habiru or Hapiru are found in cuneiform texts from different parts of the ancient Near East. According to the Tell el-Armana corre-

15

spondence, these Habiru were invading Canaan and the vassals of Egyptian Pharoah Akhnaton (c.1375-1366 B.C.) appealed frantically to him for assistance (Davis, p. 231). The meaning behind the name "Arab" has never been adequately explained, but it may be a metastasized form of Habiru and so would be identified with "nomad." This is supported by ancient south Arabian inscriptions, which associate the term with the Bedouin, the wandering herdsmen of the Arabian desert (Guillaume, p. 2)

Both the country (Ps. 72:10, 15; Isa. 21:13; Jer. 25:24; Gal. 1:17) and the people (Neh. 2:1; Isa. 13:20; Acts 2:11) are mentioned in Scripture. The first mention of the name Arab in an extra-biblical source is found in a cuneiform inscription of Assyrian king Shalmanneser III. In 853 B.C. he defeated an alliance of kings, which included king Ahab of Israel. A certain 'Jundibu the Arab' is recorded as contributing one thousand camels to the unsuccessful allied effort (ibid., p. 1).

Arabia is known primarily in Scripture under two designations: (1) *The East Country* or *the East* (Gen 25:6; 10:30; Nu. 23:7; Isa. 2:6), and (2) *The Land of the Sons of the East* (Gen. 29:1) or *Sons of the East* (Judg. 6:3; 7:12; I Ki. 4:30; Job 1:3; Isa. 11:14; Jer. 49:28 Ezek. 25:4). These terms seem to indicate the desert country east of the land of Israel, inhabited, in part, by descendants of Abraham through his son Ishmael or his concubine Keturah (Smith, Bib. Dict., p. 44). Arabic chronicles record a tribe called Katura that dwelled near the city of Mecca (Davis, p. 342).

Although modern Arabs claim descent from Abraham through Ishmael, this is hardly the case. Arabic-speaking peoples have diverse ancestries. For example, North African Arabic speakers are basically of Hamitic descent. However, Europeans began to migrate to North Africa from several sources. First of all, many Greek city states established colonies in the region beginning in the 7th century B.C. Secondly, during the Roman period North Africa received a steady stream of settlers from the Italian Peninsula and other parts of Europe. After the collapse of the Roman Empire, an-eighty-thousand-strong Germanic tribe known as the Vandals invaded Rome's North African provinces in 429 A.D. and established a kingdom there that endured for over a century (Hallett, p. 120). The Greeks returned to the region as Byzantine administrators, merchants, settlers, and soldiers beginning in 535 A.D. Also, a huge number of European captives were enslaved by Muslim pirates operating from North Africa during the Middle Ages and up until the early 19th century. Female captives often became wives and concubines of their Muslim captors. Enslaved European males were sometimes set free if they converted to Islam. Many did so. They took North African wives and raised families (Lawson, pp. 73-76). European peoples are descendants of Noah through Japheth (Gen. 10:2-5). Only a tiny percent (if any) of those who identify themselves as Arabs in this region are actually of pure Arab descent. The DNA samples of ancient Egyptians mummies and of the modern Arabic-speaking inhabitants of Egypt are nearly identical. Egypt was originally settled by Mizraim, a descendant of Noah's son Ham (Gen. 10:6).

Ishmael was the ancestor of a great many tribes in North Arabia and the Sinai. Ishmaelite tribes were by no means a majority of those living in the region in ancient times. However, they *were* prominent economically and politically. For this reason, peoples unrelated to them by blood began to call themselves Ishmaelites. There is a religious motive involved here as well, because of the spiritual reputation of Ishmael's father Abraham (Davis, p. 272).

Muhammed used the good name of Abraham to assert the primacy of Islam over both Judaism and Christianity. He claimed the patriarch was a Muslim. Indeed, it was Abraham's submission to the ultimate test of offering his son in sacrifice (described in the Quran by the verb *aslama*) that likely gave the religion of Islam its name (Smith, p. 194). However, the Quran incorrectly identifies the son as Ishmael. The Bible says Abraham "bound Isaac his son, and laid him on the altar...and took the knife to slay his son" (Gen. 22:10, 11). Also, in order to hallow a heathen sanctuary in Mecca (the Kaaba) and make it fit for Muslim use, Muhammed made up a story out of whole cloth that Abraham and Ishmael visited the place and originally reared up that sanctuary. An ancient heathen rite—the pilgrimage to Mecca—became a pillar of Islam by another stroke of Muhammed's revisionism. According to the Quran (sura 2:25), Abraham initiated the pilgrimage there (Guillaume, p. 70). However, there is absolutely no historical evidence whatever to assert that either

Abraham or Ishmael ever visited Mecca. In fact, with the possible exception of the queen of Sheba (see II Chron. 9:1-13), no biblical figure ever traveled to that city. Travelers heading north from Sheba would certainly refresh themselves at Mecca's famed well of Zamzam. However, the wise and beautiful monarch could have traveled to Israel by ship and transferred her gifts for Solomon onto a camel caravan at Eloth, Israel's southern port. After all, she ruled over a people who were also accomplished mariners.

According to the Bible, the true father of the Arabs was Joktan (Gen. 10:25-30; I Chron. 1:19-23). Even the names of his sons are found associated with geographical locations in Arabia today, such as Sheba, Ophir, Havilah, etc. Also, Abraham's nephew Lot contributed a fair share of Arab descendants, as did Jacob's brother Esau. We have already mentioned Abraham's third wife Keturah, who gave birth to six sons, who also became the ancestors of still more Arabian tribes (Shorrosh, p. 208).

III. Pre-Islamic Paganism

The claim by Muslims that their religion was given to Muhammed uncorrupted from the mind of Allah cannot be sustained. It is obvious Islam is a syncretistic stew composed of a number of diverse elements. A major ingredient of that stew is pre-Islamic paganism. All of the primitive aspects of Islam—its symbols, rituals, and festivals—were taken directly from the ancient pagan Arab religion. Pre-Islamic Arabs even referred to the Moon-god, the chief of their deities, as "Allah" (Morey, 1994, p. 15).

The Quran also mentions three goddesses worshipped by pre-Islamic Arabs: Allat (the Sun), al-Uzza (the planet Venus), and Manat (Fortune). Incidentally, Allat is merely the feminine form of Allah. Allah means "the god"; Allat means "the goddess" (Guillaume, p. 7). This is further evidence that the god of Islam was originally not the God of Abraham, but the lunar deity worshipped by the ancient Arabs and other Semitic peoples. However, we will deal with this in more detail later.

Sura 6:34 of the Quran says, "There is none that can alter the Decrees of Allah." However, the precursor of Allah's decrees in ancient Arabia was the idea of Time the Destroyer, that which fixes a person's fate, try as he might to change it. Manat was the personification of this idea (ibid., p. 8). Fate the divinity became incorporated into Islam as *kismet*—the good or bad luck that determines whether a person is born to be a beggar or a king (Spencer, p. 10).

From the Hadith (the authoritative appendix to the Quran) we learn that the ancient Arabs worshipped 360 gods and goddesses at the Kaaba in Mecca. For example, there was Suwa, a goddess. There was Yaghus the Lion, Yauk the Horse, and Nasr the Eagle. There was also an image standing in front of the Kaaba to Hobal, the guardian divinity of the city of Mecca (Shorrosh, pp. 156,157).

The pre-Islamic Arabs were also animists. Gods and spirits were believed to inhabit rocks, trees, wells, etc. Offerings were made to these features.

The stones served as altars, which were drenched in the blood of sacrificial victims. Worshippers lapped at the blood or dipped their hands in it and danced wildly around the altar stone (Guillaume, p. 8).

Sacred stones were also honored with a kiss or by stroking. The Black Stone (*al Hajar al-aswad*), located in the Kaaba, is revered by Muslim pilgrims in the same manner as sacred stones were once honored in pre-Islamic times. This stone was identified as a meteorite by a nineteenth century English explorer who visited Mecca disguised as an Arab. Obviously, the Black Stone had been the fetish of the lunar deity.

Animism had such a hold on the Bedouin and other inhabitants of the Arabian Peninsula they soon lapsed back into it after Islam spread beyond the region. Arabia became a cultural backwater. The natives of the region still worshipped Allah, but also prayed to rocks, trees, and saints. This remained the state of affairs in the homeland of Islam right up until the 18th century reform movement initiated by one Muhammed ibn Abd al-Wahhab, the founder of the Wahhabi sect dominant in Saudi Arabia today (Cole, pp. 116,117).

IV. Christianity

If the "skeleton" of Islam was provided by the ancient pagan religion of Arabia, then we could say that a good deal of its "tissue" was provided by Christianity. Christianity has been associated with Arabia from the very beginning. Arabic-speaking

Jews were probably some of the earliest converts to Christianity (Acts 2:11).

In Damascus, Syria tourists can still be taken to the place in the wall where the Apostle Paul was let down in a basket in order to escape from the Nabatean king Aretas IV (II Cor. 11:32, 33). Tradition credits the Apostle Thomas with founding the church at Edessa, Iraq. Ancient Yemen had important Christian centers. In Muhammed's time two Christian tribes, the Judham and the Udhra, lived in the Hejaz region of western Arabia (Guillaume, p. 13).

The ancient divisions of Arab Christianity still exist: Eastern Orthodoxy, Monophysite (or Jacobite), and Nestorian. Eastern Orthodox Christianity did not directly contribute to the development of Islam. It is interesting to note, however, that the Orthodox monks at the Monastery of St. Catherine at the foot of Jebel Musa (Mt. Sinai) can produce a letter supposedly from the hand of Muhammed himself. The letter grants the monastery protection in perpetuity. A document such as this could explain how the monastery has remained an island of Christianity in a sea of hostility from before the Islamic era. The monastery has existed there since 520 A.D. Then again, for centuries the monks have generously shared their wheat, fruits, and olive oil with the local Bedouin, so this protection may actually have been bought (Henriques, p. 51).

Monophysitism was propagated by Eutyches, an abbot of Constantinople. He taught that Christ's divinity was such that He was not truly human. He only had the appearance of a man. In this respect

Monophysitism is similar to the Docetist heresy (I Jn. 4:2, 3). The doctrine was rejected by the fourth General Council of Chalcedon in 451 A.D. Different versions of Monophysitism continued to be taught. For example, theanthropism taught the union of Christ's two natures into a unique, third nature. The fifth General Council convened at Constantinople (553 A.D.) called upon the secular authorities to forcibly suppress Monophysitism (Qualben, p. 123). The Coptic Church of Egypt holds to this doctrine as an article of faith.

Nestorius was a presbyter at Antioch and, subsequently, Patriarch of Constantinople (428-435 A.D.). He taught a doctrine which was almost the opposite of Monophysitism. According to Nestorius, the divine and human natures of Christ were separate almost to the point of becoming two persons. Thus, certain acts were ascribed to His divine nature while others were ascribed to His human, Since the doctrine of Nestorius could seriously compromise the value of Christ's sufferings, crucifixion, and resurrection, it was declared heretical by the third General Council of Ephesus in 431 A.D. (ibid., p. 122).

Nestorian influence came into Islam from at least three sources. First of all, Waraqa ibn Nofal, Muhammed's uncle, was a Nestorian who allegedly translated parts of the Gospels into Arabic. Secondly, Muhammed came into contact with Nestorian Christians during his caravan travels to Damascus and Egypt. Nestorian monasteries were established on the caravan routes and the caravaners were frequent guests (Shorrosh, p. 155). According to tradition, while on a journey to Syria as a 12-year boy with his uncle Abu Talib, a Nestorian monk called Buhaira declared Muhammed to be a prophet of God (Guillaume, p. 31). Also, the first of Muhammed's many wives (Khadija) is supposed to have been a Nestorian.

Muhammed was also married to a Coptic (Monophysite) slave girl by the name of Maryam. She was a gift sent by the governor of Egypt to Muhammed. This governor sent Muhammed Maryam and her sister Sirin along with a white mule. Sirin was given to another. Muhammed must have learned a great deal about Bible stories and apocryphal tales from this girl, since he is reported to have spent a great deal of time with her.

Muhammed explained the existence of both Christianity and Judaism as previous attempts by Allah to establish Islam, which were corrupted by unfaithful followers. Consequently, Christ is given high place in Islam as a *rashullah* ("messenger of Allah"), but not as the Son of God. The Quran gives this explanation in denying Christ's unique Sonship: "The Messiah, the Son of Mary, is only the messenger of Allah and His Word, which He cast to Mary and a spirit from Him. So believe in Allah and His messengers and do not say, 'Three.' Far better that you desist, because Allah is One. His transcendence is such that He cannot have a Son" (sura 4:169). Muslims completely deny the Fatherhood of God because they erroneously equate it with physical generation (ibid., p. 193). Even the term "God the Father" used strictly in a metaphorical sense is also *shirk,* an

Arabic word answering in English to "blasphemy", "idolatry", "polytheism", or even "heresy."

Since Islam was from the beginning a religion based upon works-righteousness, we should not be surprised that Christ's atoning death is also repudiated. In fact, in spite of the evidence from apostolic, patristic, rabbinic, and secular sources, the Quran denies that Jesus of Nazareth was even crucified. As sura 4:155 says, "They did not kill him and they did not crucify him, but one was made to resemble him." Muslims even claim that Judas Iscariot was mistakenly crucified instead of Jesus.

Other Christian doctrines incorporated into Islam include:

The Virgin Birth (sura 19:20) The Ascension of Christ (sura 3:55) The Holy Spirit (suras 2:81 and 5:109) Angels Satan and demons (Shaytan and jinn) Heaven and Hell.

Incidentally, the Second Advent of Christ is also affirmed by Muslims, but the doctrine is not explicitly taught in the Quran. It is a popular belief among Sunni Muslims that Isa (Jesus) will someday return and destroy all infidels and restore true Islam to the world. Thus, Jesus is recognized by many Islamic commentators as the coming *Mahdi* or "guided one" (ibid., p. 121).

The Quranic name for Jesus is curious in itself. In the Arabic New Testament He is properly called "Yesu." Apparently, Muhammed began to use the term after hearing unbelieving Jews in Yathrib (Medina) call the Lord Jesus "Esau" in derision. Esau was the twin brother of Jacob, who lost his birthright and place in the covenant line. Obviously, Muhammed began to use this term of reproach without realizing it was such (Shorrosh, p. 82).

V. Judaism

It is not known precisely when Jews first settled in Arabia. It may date from right after the fall of the northern kingdom of Israel in 722 B.C. A Jewish colony was established at Seveneh in Upper Egypt by the 6th century B.C. So it does not seem improbable that Jewish exiles would have been found in many parts of Arabia during the same period.

Subsequent persecutions and exiles by Babylonians, Seleucids, and Romans pushed Jewish refugees further into Arabia. By the fourth century A.D., colonies of Jews had spread as far south as Yemen. Eventually, the industry, skill, and knowledge of Jews living in Arabia made them prosperous and economically prominent. Towns in the Hejaz had large Jewish populations. The town of Yathrib (later renamed Medinat al Nabi or Medina) had a population that was probably at least half Jewish. From 622-632 A.D. Muhammed resided in this town and learned Old Testament stories, folklore, and Talmudic tales from the Jews living there. His two Jewish wives, Raihana and Safiyya, were further sources of information regarding Judaism.

Besides Abraham and Ishmael, the Quran mentions Noah, Joseph, Moses, Joshua, David, Solomon, Elijah, Jonah, and others. However, the Quranic versions about these Old Testament figures are distorted and often bare little resemblance to what is found in Scripture. Little wonder the Meccans would accuse Muhammed of composing the Quran with the aid of story-telling foreigners (Guillaume, p. 62).

VI. Sabeanism

As monotheists and believers in the final judgment, Sabeans (along with Christians and Jews) are accorded theorectical toleration on the basis of sura 2:59: "Believers, Jews, Christians, and Sabians—whosoever believes in Allah and the Last Day and does what is right—they shall have their reward with their Lord, they have nothing to be afraid of and shall not be grieved."

The followers of this small Iraqi sect are also called "the people of St. John," since they practice ritual immersion, as did John the Baptist (Lamsa, p. 135). However, since Sabeans also worship heavenly bodies and a hierarchy of angels, the group would seem to be Persian in origin.

The ancient Sabeans fasted for thirty days every year. The fast was broken at sunset. Apparently, Muhammed borrowed these Sabean rituals and incorporated them into the Muslim Feast of Ramadan (Shorrosh, p. 159).

Chapter 2: Facts about the Founder

I. Muhammed's Ancestry, Birth, and Childhood

The exact date of Muhammed's birth is not known. Palmer gives a possible date of April 20, 571 A.D. (p. 207). All that is certain is that he was born during what Muslims call The Year of the Elephant. In that year the Ethiopians invaded the Hejaz from Yemen. They had with them a small number of elephants. Before the invasion force could reach Mecca, an outbreak of smallpox caused it to retreat. The sura called *The Elephant* refers to this, greatly embellishing the incident with supernatural elements.

Muhammed was born in the town of Mecca, also called Bekka, names which signify a place of concourse. The city was also called Umm al Qurah, "the mother of cities," indicating it was the capital or chief of Arabian cities (ibid., p. 205).

Muhammed belonged to the leading tribe of Mecca, the Quraysh. This tribe was the official guardian of the Kaaba, the heathen sanctuary venerated from antiquity mentioned earlier. The name comes from the word *kaab*, meaning simply "cube" or "square."

Qusay, an ancestor of Muhammed, made an alliance with the Benu Kenanah tribe and drove out two other tribes, the Benu Bakr and Benu Huzahah. Thus, the sanctuary came under the guardianship of the Quraysh. The Jorhamites had custody of the place before the Benu Bakr and Benu Huzahah had defeated them.

From Qusay the guardianship passed to his eldest son, Abd ad-Dar, from whom the office passed to his brother, Abd Manaf, who had four sons: Abd Shems, Hashem, al Muttalib, and Nawfal. Hashem inherited the custodial office of the Kaaba, which passed to his son, Abd al Muttalib. However, they both dissipated the family fortune such that members of a rival family, the Ommaiyeh, positioned themselves to take over the more prestigious offices associated with the shrine (ibid., pp. 206, 207).

The youngest son of Abd al Muttalib, Abd allah, married a woman by the name of Amina. She had family in Yathrib. The protection and succor provided by her family would prove to be of supreme importance for Muhammed later.

While Amina was pregnant with the future prophet, Abd allah died on a trading trip to Yathrib. After the infant's birth, she gave him out to nurse to a Bedouin woman by the name of Halima. She returned

the infant to Amina two years later, but the mother was
so delighted with his health she persuaded Halima to
keep him another two years. During this period the
child began to have epileptic fits, such that Halima
began to believe he might be possessed by *jinn*, i.e.,
evil spirits thought to inhabit waste places. Alima
convinced her to keep the child for awhile longer, but
subsequent seizures caused Halima to return the boy
a year later. When Muhammed was six, Alima took
him on a trip to visit family in Yathrib. She died on
the return trip. Muhammed was raised by his grand-
father Abd al Muttalib, and when he died two years
later, by his uncle, Abu Talib (Shorrosh, pp. 48, 49).

II. Muhammed's Epilepsy

Concerning Muhammed's epilepsy, Guillaume
expostulates:

"A past generation of Arabists, on the basis of
this tradition and accounts of the symptoms of physical distress which sometimes accompanied his utterances, advanced the theory that Muhammed was an
epileptic. The charge had been made by a Byzantine
writer long before. Such a hypothesis seems gratu-
itous, and can safely be ascribed to anti-Muhammadan
prejudice" (p. 25).

However, Islamic sources themselves indicate
Muhammed suffered periodic bouts of mania.

Palmer describes the prophet's obvious mental
anomalies in this manner:

"From youth upward he had suffered from a
nervous disorder which tradition calls epilepsy, but

31

the symptoms of which more closely resemble certain hysterical phenomena well known and diagnosed in the present time, and which are almost always accompanied with hallucinations, abnormal exercise of the mental functions, and not unfrequently with a certain amount of deception, both voluntary and otherwise" (pp. 207, 208).

III. Muhammed the Merchant and Camel Driver

As a youth Muhammed was employed (as were most young men at the time) in tending the family sheep and goat herds. At age twelve he joined his uncle Abu Talib as a merchant and camel driver and traveled to Damascus and other cities of the East.

When Muhammed was 25 years old, he became a caravaner for a wealthy widow by the name of Khadija. She was greatly impressed by his ability and before long made him an offer of marriage. Though she was 40 years old and married twice before, Muhammed agreed. Together they had two sons and four daughters. The sons both died as infants. Muhammed did not take another wife until Khadija died about 25 years later. Then, in the manner of an Oriental potentate, he began to accumulate quite a collection of wives and concubines. The total number of his wives was fifteen (Shorrosh, pp. 49-66).

Muhammed's defenders explain his many marriages as either: (1) means to cement political alliances, or (2) humanitarian acts in order to care for widows. However, plain old lust was the sole motivation for several of the prophet's marriages. Muhammed accidentally saw the unveiled face of Zaynab, the wife of his adopted son, Zeyd. He was so smitten by her beauty that Zeyd offered to divorce her so that Muhammed could have her for himself. Since this violated tribal law, the prophet refused. Nonetheless, he agreed to his adopted son's proposal after a convenient "revelation" from Allah sanctioned it. At least three other wives were acquired as part of Muhammed's pick of the spoils of war (ibid., pp. 62-65). He married his favorite wife, Ayisha, when she was only nine years old and consummated the marriage when she was but 11 years of age.

IV. Muhammed's Call and the Formative Years of Islam in Mecca

Apparently, Muhammed had been troubled about the degenerate idolatry associated with Arab heathenism since childhood. Muhammed's first biographer, ibn Ishaq, records the following incident from his childhood:

"I was told that the apostle of Allah said, as he was talking about Zayd son of Amr son of Nufayl, "He was the first to upbraid me for idolatry and forbade me to worship idols. I had come from al-Ta'if along with Zayd son of Haritha when we passed Zayd son of Amr who was in the highland of Mecca. The Quraysh had made a public example of him for abandoning their religion, so that he went out from their midst. I sat down with him. I had a bag containing meat which had been sacrificed to our idols—Zayd son of Haritha was carrying it—and I offered it to Zayd son of Amr—I was but a lad at the time—and I said, 'Eat some of this food, my uncle.' He replied, 'Surely it is part of those sacrifices of theirs which they offer to their idols?' When I said that it was, he said, 'Nephew mine, if you were to ask the daughters of Abd al-Muttalib they would tell you that I never eat of these sacrifices, and I have no desire to do so.' Then he upbraided me for idolatry and spoke disparagingly of those who worship idols and sacrificed to them, and said, 'They are worthless: they can neither harm nor profit anyone' (or words to that effect). The apostle added, 'After that I never knowingly stroked one of their idols nor did I sacrifice to them until Allah honored me with his apostleship'" (The Life of the Messenger of Allah).

Muhammed first received his "call" to be the prophet of Allah when he was about 40 years old. He was in the habit of retiring to Mt. Hira (two or three miles from Mecca) to pray and meditate. While sleeping there one night, the angel Gabriel came to him and commanded him, "Recite." (Quran comes from an Arabic word meaning "recite" or "read.") However, he received no more revelations for a period of about three years. Muslims call this time the "Fatrah" or intermission (Palmer, p. 208).

Suicidal thoughts plagued the would-be prophet at this time. He even attempted to throw himself off a precipice, but a mysterious power seemed to hold him back. At last the hoped-for revelation came and confirmed his mission. He began to preach to the people of Mecca the content of his visions, to wit, the evils of idolatry and the oneness of Allah.

Muhammed's first convert was his wife Khadija; and then his cousin Ali and Zeyd, his adopted son. A wealthy merchant, Abu Bakr, also became convinced of this new doctrine. After a time the new faith had about 40 followers (Shorrosh, p. 54).

The Meccans were at first untroubled by Muhammed's preaching. They dismissed it as mere eccentric ravings. But as the movement began to grow, the ridicule turned to hatred and opposition. Muhammed was too well connected to be directly confronted by the authorities, but the poorer followers of the movement were fair game. A group of about 100 fled to Ethiopia for a time.

During this period Muhammed composed sura 53:19 as a minor compromise to heathenism: "Allat, al-Uzza, and Manat are the exalted ladies whose intercession is to be counted on." He later repudiated the lines as having been inspired by *Shaytan*. Salmon Rushdie's novel Satanic Verses, based on these lines, caused a worldwide jihadist furor among Muslims in February, 1989 (ibid., p. 55).

Muhammed himself was in no immediate danger, since he was under the protection of his uncle, Abu Talib. Even though Abu Talib never embraced his nephew's religion, he had great affection for Muhammed and was successful in interceding for him before the *Mala'*, the ruling council of Mecca. However, ten years after his call (c.620 A.D.), Muhammed's wife, Khadija, and his uncle Abu Talib, died within weeks of each other. Muhammed was now bereft of his relative immunity from persecution. The stage is now set for his departure from Mecca (Nigosian, p. 421).

V. The Hegira

The Kaaba received annual pilgrims from Yathrib, as it did from all parts of Arabia. A number of them accepted the new faith and shared its precepts with the folks back home. The seed of Muhammed's doctrine fell on fertile soil in Yathrib. Maternal family ties to the town would also give him a great deal of influence there.

The city was unsettled by intertribal warfare and was in need of a mediator to end the strife. Muhammed seemed like the logical choice for the job. He met with a delegation from Yathrib and won them over to his religious teaching. They then invited the prophet to come rule over them. Of course, he readily agreed. The community of his disciples preceded him to Yathrib (Smith, p. 200). Only Muhammed, his cousin Ali, and Abu Bakr remained behind in Mecca.

In the meantime the Quraysh were plotting Muhammed's assassination. It was suggested by one, Abu Gahl, that one man from each of the eleven noble families should strike him down at the same time. This stratagem would divide the responsibility and parcel out the consequences of a blood feud. It was rightly judged the Hashemites (Muhammed's family) were not powerful enough to exact vengeance on so many families and, consequently, would be forced to accept an offer of blood money instead.

Muhammed got wind of the conspiracy so he and Abu Bakr escaped by night from a rear window of the latter's house. They hid in a cave at Mt.Thaur, south of Mecca. This was a wise move, since Yathrib was some 280 miles to the northeast. For three days they hid themselves, their pursuers once coming so near the mouth of the cave a frightened Abu Bakr said, "We are but two!" "Nay," answered Muhammed, "we are three; for Allah is with us." According to the tradition, a spider wove a stout web across the mouth of the cave so that the Quraysh were fooled into thinking none had entered it and so searched elsewhere.

The two fugitives procured some fleet-footed dromedaries and reached Yathrib safely. They were joined by Ali three days later. After being jailed for a few hours, the Quraysh allowed him to leave (Palmer, pp. 210, 211).

Muhammed's escape from Mecca is known as the Hegira (*Hijra*). It took place on September 24, 622 A.D. However, the actual date was not adopted as the first day of the new era but New Year's Day of the year in which it occurred, i.e., July 15/16 622 A.D. The word *hijra* does not mean "flight" so much as a self-imposed exile involving the breaking of old ties and the making of new ones in another country (Guillaume, pp. 39, 40). The year of Muhammed's flight marks the beginning of the Muslim chronology. Thus, this year is 1 A.H. (Anno Hegira, "year of the flight") in the Muslim calendar.

VI. The First Commonwealth of the Faithful

Not long after the Hegira, the name of the city of Yathrib was changed to Medinat al Nabi ("the city of the prophet"), known commonly as Medina ("the city"). In those days the place was not actually a single city at all. It was a group of five walled towns in a shallow basin of oases, cultivated fields, and date-palm groves. Each of these towns was home to a tribe, three of which were Jewish (the Banu Qurayza, al-Nadir, and Qainuqa) and two Arab (the Aus and Khazraj).

Muhammed went about immediately to establish the first *umma,* or community of the faithful. He "proceeded to regulate the rites and ceremonies of his religion, build a mosque to serve as a place of prayer and a hall of general assembly" (Palmer, p. 211). He appointed the first *muezzin,* or crier to call the believers to their five-times-a-day devotions. This was Bilal, an Ethiopian slave who was steadfast in the face of persecution. His speech impediment has been imitated by all subsequent muezzins.

A year or two after Muhammed's arrival in Medina he drew up a charter. It reveals that the ties created by the umma transcended all other ties, even those established by blood or marriage. Thus, a believing father would have a duty to shed the blood of an unbelieving or apostate son, and visa versa. All Muslims were bound to defend and protect one another from assault by infidels. Even Jews were to receive the rights and privileges of the charter, while retaining their own religion (Guillaume, p. 41).

VII. The Genesis of Jihad

It is obvious Muhammed was encouraging Jews to become Muslims. Indeed, he probably expected them to do so. Muhammed doubtless became more and more exasperated when the vast majority of Jews obstinately refused to say of him, "Thou art the seal of the prophets." Consider the number of Jewish practices incorporated into Islam, such as circumcision, prohibition against eating pork and shellfish, and the ritual slaughter of sheep and cattle by slitting their throats and draining the blood. For a time Muhammed even commanded the *qiblah* would be toward Jerusalem. The qiblah is the direction Muslims face while in prayer (Suskind, p. 13).

It was inevitable that there would be trouble between Muhammed and his followers and the Jewish tribes. The Jews compounded their rejection of Muhammed by composing songs of derision about him. Since Muhammed could not endure such ridicule, he sent out assassins to kill the composers of these songs. No blood money was paid to the next of kin, either. As an additional sign of his displeasure with the Jews, Muhammed received yet another revelation directing the qiblah be toward Mecca.

Unfortunately for them, the Jewish tribes were suspicious of one another; they would not make common cause against the Muslims. Muhammed was able to play one tribe against the other until he was strong enough to move against them. Two of the Jewish tribes purchased their lives with their lands and possessions and were given safe passage to Syria.

The Banu Qurayza joined the Quraysh of Mecca in a war against Muhammed. The Quraysh and their allies besieged Medina but were forced to withdraw (the so-called "Battle of the Trenches"). Muhammed then, in turn, laid siege to the Banu Qurayza's town with an army of 3,000. The town surrendered at last and all of the men were beheaded (about 600) and the women and children were sold into slavery (Shorrosh, p. 67).

Muhammed was well aware of Mecca's economic vulnerability. The city was in an unproductive valley, and its inhabitants were obliged to import their own provisions. Thus, caravans were essential for Mecca's livelihood. The city's *souks, or markets*, were full of goods and foodstuffs from the Byzantine and Persian Empires. These were exchanged for ivory from Africa, incense and balsam from Yemen, and silks and spices from India.

Muhammed ordered a Qurayshite caravan to be taken. One of the drivers was killed. Though this happened in the sacred month when all warfare was banned in Arabia, Muhammed justified it with this explanation:

"They will question you regarding war during the sacred month. Tell them, "Warfare at this time is serious, indeed. Far more serious is to turn men away from Allah and to not believe in Him and His sanctuary and to drive His people from it. Idolatry is far more serious than even killing" (sura 2:214).

Muhammed planned an even larger and more daring caravan raid. Before this plan could be executed, the Quraysh sent out an escort of 1,000 mounted warriors. In the meantime Muhammed left Medina with a force of only three hundred. The two forces met at the wells of Badr (also known as Bedru) about 200 miles to the southeast of Medina in January of 624 A.D. Although the Quraysh were better armed and equipped, the zeal of the Muslims made them invincible that day. They took much plunder and a number of important prisoners. The songs around the campfires that night were all about the victory Allah had wrought through his prophet, Muhammed (Suskind, pp. 15-20).

In the East the prestige of success is bound up with notions of destiny. Indeed, Muhammed's star was rising. The former camel driver was now the master of the Hejaz. Tribal chieftains declared their allegiance to him. Singers now vied with one another to see who could compose the most laudatory anthems about the prophet.

Muhammed's victory at Badr was tarnished by defeat the next year. Three thousand Quraysh defeated a Muslim force of about 700 at Uhud, about a mile from Medina. They did not pursue their victory by occupying the town. It may have been that they thought Muhammed had been killed (he had been moderately wounded). More than likely, the Quraysh felt that honor had been satisfied and that the shame of defeat was now removed by victory, so that no further effort was necessary.

Despite the defeat and his injury, Muhammed insisted they defiantly follow the Quraysh back to Mecca. They encamped near there and built a bonfire that could be seen for miles. This act of boldness both raised the morale of the Muslims and unsettled the Qurayshites. This masterful stroke assuaged somewhat the sting of defeat (Guillaume, p. 45).

The Quraysh then prepared another expedition against Medina. Bedouin allies were enlisted and a force of 10,000 took the field. The Quraysh also made a pact with the Banu Qurayza. This Jewish tribe was supposed to make a diversionary attack, but they trusted neither the Quraysh nor their Bedouin allies, so the proposed attack never came off. The Quraysh and the Bedouin had no reason to trust one another, either. In sharp contrast with the disunity of their enemies, the Muslims were of one heart and mind.

A Persian with military experience advised Muhammed to order wide and deep trenches dug to protect the vulnerable approaches to the town. This gave the battle its name in Arabic chronicles. The Quraysh and their allies laid siege to Medina. However, Arabia was not a country for long sieges. The besiegers soon found themselves worse off than the besieged. Only one attempt was made by the Quraysh to breach the Muslim defenses, and it was handily thwarted. Discord and discouragement caused those in the camp of the besiegers to begin to drift away, first by ones and twos, and then by groups. Eventually, the camp broke up entirely and the attackers returned to their homes.

Mecca became increasingly isolated both politically and economically. Consequently, the Qurayshites were forced to sign the Treaty of Hudaybiya with Muhammed. The main provisions of the treaty were these: (1) Muslims were granted freedom of worship, (2) Muslims were permitted the right to proselytize, (3) Muhammed and his followers were allowed the right to visit the Kaaba the next year, (4) a ten-year truce was established between the Muslims and the Qurayshites, and (5) Muhammed was granted the right to make treaties with other tribes. This treaty was a tremendous diplomatic victory for Muhammed and actually accelerated Mecca's isolation.

One of the last of Muhammed's wars would eventually lead to his untimely death. He led a sneak attack against a Jewish tribe known as the Khybar. This tribe was defeated, but they were permitted to leave the Hejaz if (you guessed it!) they turned over their valuables to Muhammed. A Khaybar Jewess named Zaynab invited Muhammed and his lieutenants to dine off a lamb she prepared with poison. Only one of Muhammed's companions died, and he himself became violently ill. He would complain of the effects of the poison until he died less than four years later. Of course, Zaynab was promptly put to death (ibid., p.p. 48, 49).

As stipulated by the Treaty of Hudaybiya, Muhammed traveled to Mecca with a group of followers. The Quraysh withdrew to the hills surrounding Mecca. Muhammed promptly went to the Kaaba and circumambulated (i.e., ritually walked around) the sanctuary seven times. He entered it and touched the Black Stone with his staff. He offered sacrifices at Marwa, and the following day the prophet's muezzin stood atop the Kaaba and called the faithful to their prayers. Muhammed was allowed a three-day visit only, and though he desired to stay awhile longer, he honored the terms of the agreement and left on the fourth night.

Since Muhammed had sanctified Mecca as the center of pilgrimage for the new faith, a bone of contention that had existed between him and the Quraysh was now removed. Consequently, a number of prominent Qurayshites were won over, including a great military leader by the name of Khalid. The struggle for the holy city was now essentially at an end. Muhammed had only to bide his time and wait for a propitious moment to move on the place. It came in 8 A.H. (630 A.D.). The Quraysh broke their treaty with Muhammed and attacked a tribe allied to him. Muhammed led an army of 10,000 against Mecca and occupied the city. There was little opposition. Muhammed ordered the 360 images in and around the Kaaba to be destroyed. He demanded the key of the sanctuary from the Ommaiyeh and returned it to the rightful Hashemite custodian. He appointed his uncle Abbas as guardian of the well Zamzam. Only four of his enemies were executed. One was a poetess who composed verses satirizing the prophet (ibid., pp. 50, 51).

VIII. The Last Days of Muhammed

Muhammed made his last pilgrimage to Mecca in March of 632 A.D. He stood atop Mt. Arafat and addressed some 40,000 assembled pilgrims. He admonished them to "stand firm by the faith that he taught them, and called God to witness that he had delivered his message and fulfilled his mission" (Palmer, p. 213).

He became so ill in June of the same year that he understood his life was drawing to a close. He felt well enough on Monday the 8th of June to go to the mosque at Medina, where Abu Bakr was officiating the worship before a large assembly of those who came to hear news concerning the prophet's health. In spite of his weakness, he mounted the lower steps of the pulpit and addressed the people a few parting words. He then gave some final instructions to one Osama, who was to lead a jihadist military expedition into Syria. Muhammed then went home and there died in the arms of his beloved Ayisha (ibid., p. 214).

IX. Evaluation of Muhammed

The Quran and a great many Orientalist scholars paint a sanitized picture of Muhammed as wise, generous, a brilliant strategist, and more often than not, magnanimous to his enemies. However, the Hadith, the authoritative tradition about what the prophet or his companions said, did, or allowed, gives a different and, probably, more accurate view of Muhammed. The Hadith reveals a man more akin to a David Koresh or Jim Jones than a saint. It shows him to be steeped in pagan magic, superstitious, suspicious, vengeful, easily angered, and hungry for power. How different is this picture than that of the Lord Jesus Christ, whose moral perfection, humility, and humanity have been attested to by both His followers and enemies alike.

Chapter 3: The Subsequent History of Islam

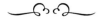

I. The First Caliph

Abu Bakr, Muhammed's trusted companion and Ayisha's father, was elected to be the Prophet's caliph. The word *khalifa* means "successor", "deputy", or "representative." The choice of this man to succeed Muhammed is the source of the eventual division of Islam into two camps. According to the Sunnis (the "orthodox" or "traditionalist" party), Muhammed left no successor. On the other hand, the Shiites (the "sectarian" or "partisan" party) claim that Muhammed actually designated his cousin Ali to be the Caliph (Nigosian, p. 424).

II. The Apostasy

Abu Bakr had such a reputation for being pious and frugal he was known as "Abu the Upright." He could also be a decisive and ruthless leader. How he dealt with the situation known as "The Apostasy" which followed the Prophet's death reveals this aspect of the man's character.

Many Arab tribes believed their allegiance to Islam ended with Muhammed's death. A number of tribal leaders declared themselves to be the true prophets of Allah. Some tribes turned back to worshipping their old familiar idols. Others were content to remain Muslims, but refused any longer to pay the alms-tax to the theocratic government at Medina (Suskind, pp. 24, 25).

Abu Bakr was incensed. "Not so much a short length of old cord will be deducted from the alms-tax," he declared. The caliph sent an army under the command of Khalid ibn al-Walid to put down the apostates. The campaign to restore the writ of the Islamic theocracy provoked further fighting that would spread to other parts of the Arabian Peninsula and beyond (Guillaume, p. 79).

Within a year the rebellion was put down. The vast majority of the apostates were pardoned, but many were executed, and some of these quite brutally. But the restoration of theocratic authority was not cheaply bought. At an oasis known as the Garden of Death, two thousand Muslims were slain in battle. So many of the *ashab*, or "Companions of the Prophet," were killed that the Quran was in danger of being lost, since most of Muhammed's visions and utterances had not been written down. Some of Muhammed's sayings were recorded on palm leaves, stones, or the shoulder-blades of animals, but many existed only in the memories of the Companions. A disciple by

Compiler of Koran

the name of Zeyd collected as many of the Prophet's words as he could from the surviving Companions and turned them over to Abu Bakr written out on separate pages (Suskind, p. 25). After further editing and revision, this material would become the Quran.

III. The Islamic Empire

The War of The Apostasy brought Khalid's army to the banks of the Euphrates. The cities of Anbar and Hira were subjugated. Hira was the seat of an Arab-Christian kingdom that managed to survive under the shadow of the Persian Empire. Its king was slain and his son was sent to Medina as a hostage. The chiefs and nobles of the former kingdom declared their allegiance to the caliph and agreed to turn over to him an annual tribute of seventy thousand pieces of gold (Gibbon, p. 218).

Khalid shifted his theater of operations to Syria. Damascus was sacked by his army in 634 A.D. after a march across the desert. The arrival of a Byzantine army forced Khalid to withdraw, but two years later the Muslims inflicted such a serious defeat on the Byzantines at the Yarmouk River that nearly all of Syria and Palestine fell like ripe fruit into Muslim hands (Guillaume, p. 79). In the meantime, the invasion of the Persian frontier was placed in the hands of less competent commanders. Consequently, a Muslim attempt to cross the Euphrates was repulsed with great loss. A Persian attempt to pursue the Muslims back into Arabia was badly mauled, so that the army of the caliph remained close to Persian territory in the desert of Iraq (Gibbon, p. 219).

The chronic divisions that heretofore plagued the Persian Empire were put aside. The Persian nobility deposed the Empress Arzema and presented the crown to a fifteen-year-old prince, Yezdegerd. The command of the army was given to an experienced general by the name of Rustem. He collected a polyglot force of 120,000 subjects, allies, and mercenaries. Rustem's army outnumbered that of the Muslims three or four to one. However, the moral advantages of discipline and unity belonged to the Muslims. So when the two forces met on the plain of Kadesia on the west bank of the Euphrates in April of 637, it was a touch-and-go affair.

Arab chroniclers describe the battle of Kadesia according to a particular incident or characteristic during a certain day of fighting. Gibbon explains:

"The first, from the well-timed appearance of six thousand of the Syrian brethren, was denominated the day of *succor*. The day of *concussion* might express the disorder of one, or perhaps of both, of the contending armies. The third, a nocturnal tumult, received the whimsical name of the night of *barking*, from the discordant clamours, which were compared to the inarticulate sounds of the fiercest animals. The morning of the succeeding day determined the fate of Persia; and a seasonable whirlwind drove a cloud of dust in the faces of the unbelievers. The clangor of arms was re-echoed to the tent of Rustam, who, far unlike the ancient hero of his name, was gently reclining in a cool and tranquil shade, amid baggage of his camp, and the train of mules that were laden with gold and silver. On the sound of danger he started from his couch, but his flight was overtaken by a valiant Arab, who caught him by the foot, struck off his head, hoisted it on a lance, and instantly returning to the field of battle, carried slaughter and dismay among the thickest ranks of the Persians" (p. 220).

The battle was decisive. A few months later the Persian capital of Ctesiphon (or Madayn) fell. A city which had successfully resisted Roman siege engines! Yezdegerd fled to his territories in the northwest. The Muslims pursued him, conquering one satrapy after another in the process. The emperor was finally killed just outside the city of Merv in 652 A.D. (Suskind, pp. 29-32).

The Muslim conquest of Egypt took place under Caliph Omar the Great (634-644 A.D.). It was a relatively easy conquest, since the Orthodox Byzantines ruled over their Coptic subjects harshly. In early 639 Amru led a force of 10,000 across the Sinai desert into Egypt. The native Copts joined forces with Amru and assisted him in clearing the Byzantines from the country within a couple of years.

The Muslim occupation of conquered lands followed the same pattern. Since Omar feared his troops would become corrupt if allowed to socialize with subject peoples, he ordered them to live apart in camps on the edge of the desert where no town previously existed. These towns became administrative centers. Although the practice would be discontinued by later caliphs, some of these camps became important cities: Basra (Iraq), Cairo (Egypt), and Kairoun

(Tunisia). Some of these camps were abandoned and are now ruins, such as Kufa in Iraq.

Non-Muslims belonging to "tolerated" religions, referred to as *dhimmis*, were forced to pay a special tax, the *jizya*, indicating second-class citizenship and subjugation to the umma. This policy quite naturally led to vast conversions to Islam. These converts became "Arabs" by making themselves wards (*mawali*) of some Arab tribe (Guillaume, p. 80).

Omar was assassinated by a dirk-wielding Persian slave, while praying at a mosque at Medina in November of 644. A council elected Othman to succeed him. Othman would occupy the caliphate from 644-656. He belonged to one of the old ruling families of Mecca, the Ommaiyeh. Othman practiced nepotism. Thus, he packed the most important offices of the empire with his relatives. Many of these office-holders were either incompetent or just downright corrupt. The discontent caused by this nepotism would eventually turn into open rebellion. An army from Basra and Kufa marched on Medina and demanded Othman abdicate. When he refused, the rebels stormed his house and murdered the caliph.

Ali was elected to succeed Othman. He was the fourth and last of the "Rightly Guided Claiphs," sometimes also called "the Barefoot Caliphs." This revived the old clan rivalry between the Hashemites and the Ommaiyids of Mecca noted in the last chapter. This rivalry would develop into the schism that would finally rend Islam. Muhammed's widow, Ayisha, opposed Ali's appointment, as did two other important Muslim leaders called Talha and Zarbayr.

Although Ali was able to defeat and kill these two in the so-called "battle of the camel," the victory did not settle the matter.

Ali attempted to depose one Muawiza as governor of Syria. Muawiza was Othman's nephew, and since the man was both ambitious and anxious to avenge his uncle's death, he refused to resign. Ali tried to forcibly remove Muawiza. The two factions fought an indecisive battle at Siffin on the banks of the Euphrates. An attempt to negotiate a third-party settlement aroused the ire of a group of fanatics against Ali. They felt that Muhammed's successor had no need to submit to such arbitration, as if the will of Allah could be decided by human courts and judges! They formed a third party known as the Suceders or *Kharijites*. Ali would not have an easy time suppressing this faction. In the meantime, a negotiated settlement favored Muawiza, but Ali refused to accept it. Muawiza then established a rival caliphate based in Damascus, and even added Egypt to his dominions. On January 20, 661 Ali was assassinated by a Kharijite while walking to the mosque at Kufa. Hassan, his son, refused to be caliph and assigned all such claims to Muawiza, who became the first caliph of the Ommaiyid dynasty (ibid., pp. 80-82).

The Ommaiyid dynasty witnessed the continued expansion of the Muslim empire. Under Caliph Othman the first military expedition (in 647 A.D.) was launched against *al-Maghrib*, "The West," termed North Africa or Barbary by Europeans. This "Wild West of Araby" was subdued only after seventy years of difficult fighting against some of the fiercest of tribes, the Berbers. Since many of these Berber tribesmen would become Kharijites, their struggle against Sunni Arab domination would continue well into the next century (Hallett, pp.120, 121).

The struggle for the caliphate would also continue during this period. A few years after Ali's assassination, his son Hassan died. Shiites insist that he was poisoned by one of Muawiza's agents. His younger brother Hussein lived an uneventful life during Muawiza's reign. However, when Muawiza's son Yezid succeeded him as caliph, Hussein asserted his claim to the office. He set out for Kufa with a small force of 200. On October 10, 680 a much larger force of Yezid's warriors surrounded and massacred Hussein and his entire group at Karbala, Iraq. His severed head was sent to Damascus as a trophy. Later, it was buried with the body at Karbala. The 10th of Muharran (the first month of the Muslim year) commemorates this day, which ends a ten-day time of lamentation observed yearly by Shiites. Forty days later a passion play called "The Return of the Head" is enacted at Karbala (Guillaume, p. 116).

The Muslim conquest of Spain was a direct result of the conquest of Barbary by the armies of this new faith. The Visigoth kings of Spain held the fortress of Ceuta on the Moroccan coast near the channel dividing the European and African continents. Musa, the military governor or *amir* of the Maghgrib, made an unsuccessful attempt to breach the walls of Ceuta. The place would fall to Musa, not by clash of arms, but due to the treachery of Ceuta's commander, Count Julian. His treason is defended by many Spaniards as stemming from the man's desire to avenge the rape of his daughter Cava by Rederic, the Visigoth king of Spain (Gibbon, pp. 227, 228). More than likely, Count Julian's treachery was purchased by bribes of gold and by the promises of the lands and booty that would surely be distributed by his new Muhammedan masters.

The condition of the country prior to the Muslim conquest could aptly describe that of other lands now under the Banner of the Crescent Moon:

"The Goths were no longer the victorious barbarians who had humbled the pride of Rome, despoiled the queen of nations, and penetrated from the Danube to the Atlantic Ocean. Secluded from the world by the Pyrenean mountains, the successors of Alaric had slumbered in long peace; the walls of the cities were mouldered into dust; the youth had abandoned the exercise of arms; and the presumption of their ancient renown would expose them in a field of battle to the first assault of the invaders" (ibid., p. 229).

In 711 a Muslim army under a Berber general named Tarik landed opposite Ceuta at a place that would bear his name—*Jebel al-Tarik*—"the mountain of Tarik," since corrupted into the familiar Gibraltar. His army numbered 12,000. King Roderic gathered an army of about 25,000 and met Tarik in battle near the town of Cadiz. Roderic had the numerical advantage, but he was hated by some of his nobles. At a critical time during the battle these nobles abandoned the field with all their troops. This turned the tide of battle in favor of Tarik, so that Roderic and the greater part of his remaining troops died in the fighting. By 713 nearly all of the Iberian Peninsula was in Muslim hands. Only a mountainous stronghold in the northwest held out under the semi-legendary Visigoth chief Pelayo (Suskind, p. 53).

IV. The Defeat, Decline, and Dissolution of the Arab Empire

If a gambling syndicate existed in the 8th century and was taking bets on the outcome of the coming struggle between Islam and the Christian West, no doubt the bets would have overwhelmingly favored Islam. In the century that had passed since the death of Muhammed and the battle of Tours (732 A.D.), "the followers of the Prophet had torn away half the Roman Empire; and besides their conquests over Persia, the Saracens had over run Syria, Egypt, Africa, and Spain, in an uncheckered and apparently irresistible career of victory" (Creasy, p. 183).

Nor were the chiefs
Of victory less assured, by long success
Elate, and proud of that o'erwhelming strength
Which, surely they believed, as it had roll'd
Thus far uncheck'd, would roll victorious on,
Till, like the Orient, the subjected West
Should bow in reverence at Mohammed's name;
And pilgrims from remotest Arctic shores
Tread with religious feet the burning sands
Of Araby and Mecca's stony soil.
(Southey-*Roderic*)

Furthermore, Abderrahman, the amir of Andalusia (Spain), was an able commander of a first-rate army of 80,000, which included a picked force of Berber cavalry.

On the other hand, The Merovingian kings of Gaul (the country had not yet become France) had become mere decadent puppets dominated by their stewards known as the Mayors of the Palace. Fortunately for Western Civilization, the current Mayor of the Palace was Charles Martel (i.e., "Charles the Hammer"), an equally skilled leader and man of war from his youth.

The Muslims were initially successful in their invasion of Gaul. They defeated a number of locally raised armies and gathered much plunder and many captives as they spread through Provence. This Arab love of booty would be the undoing of their enterprise, according to their own chronicles:

"Near the River Owar (i.e. the Loire), the two great hosts of the two languages and the two creeds were set in array against each other. The hearts of Abderrahman, his captains, and his men, were filled with wrath and pride, and they were the first to begin the fight. The Moslem horsemen dashed fierce and frequent forward against the battalions of the Franks, who resisted manfully and many fell dead on either side, until the going down of the sun. Night parted the two armies; but in the gray of the morning the Moslems returned to battle...But many of the Moslems were fearful for the sake of the spoil which they had stored in their tents, and a false cry arose in their ranks that some of the enemy were plundering the camp; whereupon several squadrons of the Moslem horsemen rode off to protect their tents" (Don Jose Conde, <u>History of Arab Rule in Spain</u>, 1820; translation of original Arab account).

The sight of so many of their companions leaving caused others in the Muslim battle-line to believe they were in retreat. As Abderrahman personally attempted to stem this tide with loud expostulations, he was killed by an onrush of Christian spearmen (Creasy, p. 189).

The rout at Tours was so complete, the same Arab chronicles admit it was "the disgraceful overthrow." No other serious attempt at conquest beyond the Pyrennes was made by the Muslims. This single battle, as one writer says, "Rescued our ancestors of Britain and our neighbors of Gaul from the civil and religious yoke of the Koran" (ibid., p. 179). Charles Martel, the victor of Tours, would go on to found a dynasty that would resurrect the Roman Empire under his grandson Charlemagne.

Shortly after this defeat the old fued between the Hashemite and Ommaiyid clans broke out anew. A faction of the Hashemites descended from Muhammed's uncle Abbas gathered a largely Persian army and placed it under the command of a man called Ibrahim. This force defeated the Ommaiyids on the banks of the River Zab in 750. The new dynasty is called the "Abbasid" after the name of the aforementioned Abbas. Hashemite retribution against their Ommaiyid foes was so terrible that the first Abbasid caliph has been called "Abu the Bloody" (Suskind, p. 62).

However, surviving Ommaiyids made their way to Spain, gathered an army there under Abdul Rahman, overthrew the Abbasid governor, and established a new Ommaiyid dynasty. Muslim Spain was thereafter known as the Western Caliphate.

The Abbasids moved their capital from Damascus to Baghdad. Under Caliph Haroun al-Raschid (786-809), Islamic civilization reached its pinnacle. However, the Abbasid caliphs began to depend more and more upon mercenaries from Turkistan. Apart from religion, the Arabs had nothing in common with the Turks from this region in Central Asia. The Turkish mercenaries were little more than hired thugs who took whatever they wanted from the Arabs. In turn, the Arabs would fall upon any stray Turk they could find and murder him. There was so much bad blood between these two races that Caliph Mutasim moved the capital to Samarra, some 80 miles further up the Tigris. This move not only isolated the caliph from his subjects, but it would turn those Turkish mercenaries into a kind of Praetorian Guard, dethroning Abbasid caliphs at will. The commander of the Turkish bodyguard, beginning with Bugha in 861, became virtual rulers. The Abbasid caliphs were now mere puppets. In the meantime, the empire disintegrated as independent rulers established themselves in Tunisia, Egypt, Syria, and Persia (ibid., pp. 69, 70).

It was a Turkish tribe known as the Seljuks who actually provoked the Crusades. In 1070 they swept over Syria and Palestine, capturing Jerusalem. They desecrated churches and robbed and murdered

European pilgrims. So it was the desire to protect pilgrims and restore their free access to holy sites in Palestine, and not Christian imperialism (as is commonly asserted), that was the initial motivation behind European intervention in the Holy Land.

Between 1096 and 1291 there were a total of eight ecclesiastically sanctioned military expeditions to the Holy Land:

First Crusade (1096-1099): led by Godfrey of Bouillon, Raymond of Toulouse, Robert of Flanders, and Robert of Normandy. Jerusalem was captured. The Latin Kingdom of Jerusalem (also known as Outremer, "land beyond the sea") was established.

Second Crusade (1147-1148): failed to recapture Edessa. Led by Conrad III of Germany and Louis VII of France.

Third Crusade (1189-1192): Led by Richard I ("Lion Heart") of England, Phillip II of France, and Fredrick Barbarossa of Germany. A truce was worked out with Saladin and a second Latin Kingdom of Jerusalem established.

Fourth Crusade (1201-1204): it is called the "Constantinople Crusade" because the initial objective of conquering Egypt ended with the sack of Constantinople, the Byzantine capital. Led by Philip of Swabia, Baldwin of Flanders, and Theobald III of Champagne.

Fifth Crusade (1217-1221): Andrew of Hungary and Leopold VI of Austria led an army to Palestine but failed in their objective to conquer Egypt.

Sixth Crusade (1228-1229): German Emperor Fredrick II negotiated the recovery of Jerusalem, Nazareth, and Bethlehem. In 1266 Baibars, the future Mameluke Sultan of Egypt, recaptured Jerusalem.

Seventh Crusade (1248): led by Louis IX of France. His army was routed near Cairo. In 1250 he reached Acre, where he remained four years fortifying Haifa, Caesarea, Jaffa, and other costal towns. Most Crusader strongholds were destroyed by Baibars in 1263.

Eighth Crusade (1270): Louis IX (later St. Louis) and the future Edward I of England attempted to conquer Tunis (St. Louis would die at Carthage). In 1271 Prince Edward led an unsuccessful Crusade to Acre. Acre was the last Crusader stronghold to fall in 1291, captured by Baibars' grandson.

As these invasions were taking place from the West, tribal groups continued to attack the lands of the Abbasid Caliphate from the steppes of Central Asia. The Ghaznavids from Afghanistan raided Iraq. The Mongols sacked Baghdad and accomplished the final overthrow of the Abbasid dynasty there in 1258. Though these savage warriors would eventually embrace Islam under Ghazan Khan (1255-1304), it would not be the Mongols of Iraq who would restore the jihadist glory of Islam's early days. That task would fall to the Ottoman Turks, the last dynasty to hold the Caliphate (Nigosian, p. 429).

V. The Ottoman Empire (c.1299-1922)

The Turkish conquest of Anatolia began with the crushing defeat of the Byzantine armies of Romanus II Diogenes at the battle of Manzikert by Alp Arslan in 1071. The Ottoman state was one of many petty principalities which grew out of this conquest. It gained regional dominance, especially after the main Seljuk state, the Sultanate of Konya, became a vassal of the Mongol Khans. The Ottoman state was composed of restless warriors, who were more at home on their horses, which they called "sons of the wind," than becoming peaceful agriculturalists.

By 1353 the Ottomans landed on the European side of the Hellespont. In 1389 they broke the power of Serbia at the battle of Kosovo. Not even the defeat of Sultan Bayazid by Tamerlane in 1402 could do anything but put a temporary halt to the expansionist plans of the Ottomans. The last remnants of the mighty Byzantine Empire, an enclave around the city of Constantinople, fell to Sultan Mehemet II in 1453.

Although the Ottoman Empire was theoretically ruled by sharia, in practice, the Sultan was bound by it only as much as he desired. The political theory of the sultans was based on absolute autocracy. Since each prince was a potential candidate for the throne, each new sultan made sure all of his brothers were put to death.

The Ottomans became militant defenders of Sunni Islam because of the rise of the Shiite Safavid dynasty in Persia in 1502. Missionaries and agents from there disseminated doctrines which appealed to the Anatolian Turks. As a consequence, intense persecution of Shiites began throughout the Sultanate. Also, foreign conquests were undertaken in order to spread Sunni Islam. In this way, Syria, Egypt, and North Africa (except Morocco) came under Ottoman rule. A titular Abbasid caliph had been installed by the Mamelukes at Cairo, Egypt. However, with the Ottoman conquest of the country in 1517, the Ottoman Sultans could truly claim to be the actual leaders and champions of orthodox (i.e., Sunni) Islam.

Constant warfare against Safavid Persia saved a Europe divided by sectarian violence from being completely overrun by the Ottomans. Even so, under Suleiman I, "The Magnificent," a Hungarian army was destroyed at Mohacs in 1526. The Hungarian King Louis II was killed and Hungary lost its independence for more than a century. Suleiman's victory further enabled him to threaten Austria and Central Europe in 1529. It was only the premature onset of winter that forced him to withdraw from his siege of Vienna in October of the same year. A second Ottoman attempt to dominate Central Europe was thwarted as a result of the Ottoman defeat during the Great Turkish War (1683-1699). The second siege of Vienna (1683) ended in failure. The Turkish commander, Grand Vizier Kara Mustafa, was executed for his failed attempt to capture the city. At the second battle of Mohacs (August, 1687), the Ottomans were decisively defeated and driven from Hungary. The Ottomans under Sultan Mustafa II were decisively defeated a third time at Zenta (80 miles north of Belgrade) by Austrians under Prince Eugene of Savoy on September 11, 1697 (Perrett, pp. 207, 208; pp. 302, 303; p. 329). Thereafter, the fortunes of the Ottoman Empire would decline.

In the 18th century the technological gap between Europe and the Ottoman Empire grew wider. Consequently, European military power became superior to that of the Ottoman Sultanate. During the same period Russia began to expand at the expense of the Ottoman Empire. The sultan sought an alliance, especially with England and France. To achieve this the sultan was forced to pay a heavy price in concessions to these powers. Once the terror of Europe, the Ottoman Empire came to be called, "the sick man of Europe."

Throughout the 19th century the Ottoman Empire continued to lose its European territories. During World War I the sultan allied his country with the Central Powers. Revolts and Allied invasions stripped the sultan of his Arab territories. Finally, a revolt by Kemal Ataturk in 1922 put an end to the Ottoman Empire. On March 3, 1924 the National Assembly of the newly proclaimed Republic of Turkey voted to abolish the caliphate. In dealing the death blow to this institution, Ataturk said, "The idea of a single caliph, exercising supreme religious authority over all the peoples of Islam, is an idea taken from fiction, not from reality." With that, Caliph Abdul Majid, the last Ottoman to hold the office, was sent into exile (Nigosian, p. 434).

Chapter 4: The Teachings of Islam

I. The Articles of Faith

Sura 2:176 summarizes the Islamic articles of faith: "Verily piety is this: to believe in Allah, the Judgment Day, angels, the Book, and the prophets." Predestination is also an important basic doctrine of the religion.

The Oneness of Allah

Since Muhammed borrowed freely from Judaism and heretical forms of Christianity, we should not be surprised that Islam would stress the absolute unity of Allah. He was sure the Christian doctrine of the Trinity was actually tritheism, and so declared it to be *shirk*, i.e., the sin of "associating" (an unforgivable form of heresy).

Allah possesses all the "omnis"—omniscience (all-knowing), omnipotence (all-powerful), and omnipresence (existing everywhere). The Quran also teaches he is the eternal Creator of the universe. Although again and again this book refers to him as "the compassionate and merciful," the biblical idea of a God who saves by grace according to His unmerited and undeserved favor is entirely absent. Furthermore, as McDowell points out, Allah is not knowable in a personal sense. "The goal of Islam," he observes, "is to obey Allah, not to know him" (p. 115).

The Judgment Day

It is obvious the Quranic teaching concerning the Judgment Day is taken from Christian and Jewish sources. On that Day (the time of which is known only to Allah), a trumpet will sound and the graves will be opened. The risen dead will have their deeds weighed in a balance. A record-book of one's life will be given to each. Muslims will receive the book in the right hand, indicating they will enter paradise (though some must be purged of their sins). All others will be given the book in the left hand, which means they will be doomed to hell.

Angels and Spirits

Belief in angels is an essential one in Islam since it was the Archangel Gabriel who revealed himself to Muhammed. Besides Gabriel (the revealer), there are three other archangels: (1) Michael (the angel of providence), (2) Israfil (the angel of destruction),

and (3) Izrail (the angel of death). There are minis-
tering angels who act as guardian spirits, record-
keepers, interrogators of the dead, etc. (Shorrosh., p.
29). Another class of being is intermediate between
angels and men, the *jinn*. These beings were created
out of fire. There are both good and bad jinn. Solomon
received occult knowledge from them. Others are
sometimes referred to as *shaytans* and their lord is
"the Shaytan" or *Iblis*, a corruption of the Greek
word *diobolos* or devil (Guillaume, p. 65).

The Quran

There are four books of Scripture recognized
by Muslims: (1) the Torah or Law of Moses, (2) the
Psalms of David, (3) the *Injil* or Gospel of Jesus,
and (4) the Quran. The Quran is regarded as the final
revelation of Allah, abrogating all previous revelations. What Muslims call the Law, the Psalms, and
the Gospel are not those recognized by Christians
and Jews. Muslims claim (without the slightest bit of
evidence) that the Law, the Psalms, and the Gospel
have been hopelessly corrupted and are now lost.
Actually, there is no substantial difference between
the most ancient Biblical manuscripts. If the text
of Scripture had been so badly corrupted so early,
as Muslims assert, the ancient manuscripts would
greatly vary. The differences between the texts are
so minor that no doctrine of Scripture is affected. We
can be more confident in the text of the Bible than in
any other book from the ancient world (Strobel, pp.
70-93).

The Muslim boast that the Quran as it now exists is letter for letter the same document that Allah gave to Muhammed does not stand up to historical scrutiny. (The notion of an uncorrupted Quran is used as an argument to prove its divine origin.) As noted in the previous chapter, the haphazard collection of Muhammed's words was gathered up by Zeyd and turned over to Abu Bakr. This collection came into the possession of Caliph Omar's daughter Hafsa (one of Muhammed's widows). From this material at least four rival editions of the Quran came into use. Caliph Othman assembled a commission (in which Zeyd played a leading part) and they prepared a text that all Muslims were commanded to accept. The *ulama* (religious authorities) of Kufa were adamant in refusing this "authorized" edition and continued to use one of their own. As late as 1000 A.D. copies of this unofficial edition could still be found. Even to this day variant readings can be found in Quranic texts not only in the readings of vowels, but even in the consonantal text (Guillaume, pp. 57, 58).

Another Muslim "proof" of the Quran's divine origin is that as literature it is without equal. However, great literature will come through even in translation. Anyone who has read through the Bible, Homer, or Virgil would agree. Although the Quran is surely an important document, it does not measure up to being classified a literary masterpiece. Therefore, Thomas Carlyle's assessment of it is completely correct: "It is as toilsome reading as I ever undertook, a wearisome, confused jumble, crude, incondite. Nothing but a sense of duty would carry any European through the

Koran" ("The Hero as Prophet," <u>Heroes and Hero-Worship</u>, 1900; quoted by Smith, p. 203).

The reason the Quran seems a confused jumble in translation is because it is disorganized in the classical Arabic original. A complete discourse on any given subject can hardly be found in any single sura. If the Quran came directly from Allah, surely it would have been given perfectly organized.

Another argument advanced by Muslims as proof of the Quran's divine origin seems almost childish. Since Muhammed was illiterate, they point out, only a miracle could have "produced a book embodying all wisdom and theology essential to human life" (Smith, p.203). However, illiterate poets in oral societies (as was 7th century Arabia) are capable of extemporaneous composition and recitation of poems of prodigious length. Some of these poems, also known as epics, are 12,000 or more lines in length (Dundes, p. 268). The Quran's 6,200 or more verses is well within the range of an oral poet's capabilities. The effortless way these epic singers ply their craft might give one the impression of an otherworldly inspiration, but the endeavor is entirely the product of the human mind.

The disjointed nature of the Quran would not speak well of Muhammed's ability as an oral master of epic wordsmanship. We can account for this because he obviously *could* read and write. As Prof. Lord has observed, literacy seems to dampen extraordinary oral feats aided solely by the memory (ibid. p. 268).

Traditionally, Muhammed has been termed *al-Nabi al-Ummi*, "the illiterate prophet," but should probably be more correctly translated "the gentle prophet" (Shorrosh, p. 192). Furthermore, there is much documentary evidence that Muhammed was fully literate: (1) he personally signed the Treaty of Hudaybiya, (2) on his deathbed he asked Ayisha for writing material so he could write down the name of his successor (he was too weak to do so), and (3) the personal letter he wrote to the monks at St. Catherine's monastery mentioned earlier (ibid., pp. 52, 53). This by no means exhausts the evidence of Muhammed's literacy, either.

Muslims will also tell you the divine origin of the Quran is evident because it is free of grammatical errors. Again, an illiterate Muhammed could not possibly have accomplished such a thing by natural means. Yet, Dr. Shorrosh (pp. 199, 200), a Palestinian and fluent speaker of Arabic, lists grammatical faux pas in the following suras: 2:177 (The Cow), 7:160 (The Heights), 4:162 (The Women), 5:169 (The Table Spread), 63:10 (The Hypocrites), and 3:59 (The Family of Imran).

There is also the problem of a sizable portion of Allah's "eternal" word ending up as sheep droppings on some pasture outside of Medina. A *hadith* having the authority of Ayisha states that she said verses about the stoning of adulterers and about ten acts of sucking by an infant were under her bed when Muhammed died. She was so distracted in her mourning and distress that a sheep entered the house and ate the pages containing the verses. Thus, a sura now containing 73 verses originally had about 200. A 10th century Muslim writer attacked the authenticity of this tradition:

"This completely contradicts the word of Allah: 'It is a mighty scripture: a vain thing cannot come at it from the front or the rear' (41:41). But how could the Quran be mighty if a sheep ate it and made its law null and void and destroyed the very evidence of its existence? Could Allah have then declared, 'This day (the record of) your faith is made complete'—and then he sends some creature to dine on a portion of it" (Guillaume, pp. 107, 108)?

However, his very objection actually confirms the authenticity of this hadith. Knowing how Muhammed's followers esteemed his words, it is unlikely such a tradition would have been invented by one of them were it not true. And if the source of this tradition had come from outside the *umma* in order to discredit the Quran, it would have been rejected out-of-hand and would not have circulated so long after the death of the Prophet.

Prophets

Islam recognizes 28 prophets, including Muhammed. Eighteen are Old Testament figures, and these include Adam, Noah, Abraham, Ishmael, Moses, Isaac, Jacob, Joseph, David, Solomon, Elijah, Elisha, Jonah, etc. Islamic prophets found in the New Testament are Zachariah, John the Baptist, and Jesus. Curiously enough, the Quran unequivocally declares Alexander the Great to be a prophet (18:83-100, <u>The</u>

Cave). This pagan ruler was both morally corrupt and received worship as a god. Why Muhammed would include him in the company of the prophets is surely a testimony to his ignorance of history (Shorrosh, p. 194).

Predestination

As we have previously seen (Chapter 1), even pre-Islamic Arabs had notions of fate or destiny personified in the goddess Manat. The idea of fate became incorporated into the Quran in texts which assert that both the good and evil deeds men commit are decreed by Allah. Certain schools of Islamic scholarship have tried to mitigate the language of these texts. However, it cannot be denied the orthodox party not only has the Quran on their side, but also the canonical tradition, which does not contain even one of Muhammed's sayings assigning to men freedom of action (Guillaume, pp. 131, 132).

II. The Pillars of Islam (arkan al-Islam)

It should be noted particularly that the Five Pillars of Islam are far more than just teachings, but essential duties foundational for being a Muslim (Newby, p. 173). They reveal the essence of Islam's system of salvation, which is based, not on the unmerited and undeserved favor of God, but entirely on what the individual can do to please the Supreme Being. Thus, Islam does not represent progress in man's spiritual growth, but is a regression, a return to his spiritual immaturity:

"Children first learn principles of right conduct until conscience takes the place of external authority. With the race the same progress holds good. Earlier forms of religion are more external. The latest is the most spiritual. To turn away from the spiritual is not merely to go back; it is to revert to a more improper method" (Spence, p. 173).

It has been said that the major theme of the Bible is *liberty*—spiritual, social, and political. With centuries of fitful starts and stops, such has been the progress in lands where this biblical theme has been taken most seriously.

The opposite can be discerned from the Quran and its companion, the Hadith. Together they enjoin *submission* for the Muslim, *subjugation* for the dhimmi, and *death* for the polytheist. The Quran and the Hadith form a constitution for the establishment of a spiritual and political despotism so vile as to make warm the heart of Orwell's Big Brother.

The works-righteousness nature of Islam centers around the Five Pillars: (1) the *shahada*, or the recitation of the formula, "There is no god but Allah, and Muhammed is his prophet," (2) *salat*, the five daily prayers, (3) *zakat*, the giving of alms, (4) *sawn*, the keeping of the sunrise to sunset fast during the month of Ramadan, and (5) the *hajj*, making a pilgrimage to Mecca at least once in a lifetime.

Additionally, there are meticulous rules about washing, how and where to urinate and defecate, the kinds of garments and adornments one can wear, etc, that are mandatory for all the followers of Muhammed. These regulations are defined to an even greater extent than even similar duties in the Jewish Talmud (Guillaume, p. 88).

The Shahada (also the Kalima)

This is one of the shortest creeds of any religion. Muslims repeat it many times in the course of a day: "There is no god but Allah, and Muhammed is his prophet."

Salat

The Quran appears only to require three times of prayer daily. Tradition dictates five such times of devotion: the first at sunset, the second is just before bedtime, followed by dawn, noon, and afternoon prayer. The *muezzin* calls the faithful to their prayers. He climbs a tower connected to the mosque called a *minaret* and cries out in Arabic: "Allah akhbar (i.e., Allah is greatest). I testify there is no god but Allah. I testify that Muhammed is the prophet of Allah. Come to prayer. Come to security. Allah akhbar." Incidentally, the word *mosque* means "place of prostration" (ibid., p. 66).

Muslims will often go pray at the mosque. Since Muslims must face Mecca while in prayer, this direction, or *qiblah*, is indicated by a niche or recess called the *mihrab*. The prayers are recitations in Arabic of certain formulas, such as the *Fatiha*, the first sura of

the Quran. Prayers are accompanied by bowings or
rakas.

Public services are held in mosques on Fridays.
Men and women do not worship together. The
central hall is reserved for the men. Women worship
in the back of this hall or in a separate room. Before
entering a mosque, ablutions involving the washing
of hands, feet, and face must be performed. Shoes
cannot be worn inside the mosque.

Zakat

Almsgiving is both voluntary and obligatory. The
latter was collected in the early days by government
tax collectors and was set at two and one-half percent
of a man's wealth. Today the duty of charity is now
left to the conscience of the individual Muslim in
most Islamic countries. Ideally, almsgiving is to
follow a hierarchy of need beginning with slaves
attempting to buy their freedom, debtors unable to
pay their debts, wayfarers and religious pilgrims, and
those who collect and distribute the alms (Smith, p.
213).

Sawn (fasting during the month of Ramadan)

Ramadan is one of the months of the Islamic
calendar. It is Islam's holiest month because in it
Muhammed received his initial revelation and ten
years later he made his Hegira or flight from Mecca
to Medina during this month. Since Muslims use a
lunar calendar of 354 days, the month of Ramadan

eventually rotates through all the seasons of the year.

A common misconception about Ramadan is that Muslims will not initiate warfare during this sacred period. Nothing could be further from the truth. The Yom Kippur War in 1973 began with an Egyptian assault on Sinai during Ramadan. Hence, it is called the Ramadan War in the Arab world. Jihadist fanatics are just as likely to engage in terrorism during Ramadan as any other time of the year.

The fasting during the month takes place during the daylight hours. Not even water can be consumed at this time, and this can be quite a burden when Ramadan occurs during the hottest months. Most Muslims eat only two meals a day during the festival, one just after sundown and another before dawn.

The Hajj

All devout, able-bodied Muslims are required to make a pilgrimage to Mecca at least once in a lifetime. The only exceptions are invalids, slaves, and women without a male relative (women are not allowed to make the *hajj* by themselves). However, it is possible to make the trip by proxy through another pilgrim. In such a circumstance the one who stays behind must contribute to the substitute who makes the pilgrimage as much as he can afford. The proxy brings the merit upon all who made it possible (Nigosian, p. 446).

The hajj is not simply a visit to Mecca. A number of rituals and other duties must be performed. The Kaaba is located in the center of a large open-air enclosure known as the Grand Mosque. Before entering, the pilgrim must perform the necessary ablutions, remove his shoes, and put on a seamless white garment. He then approaches the Kaaba and circumambulates it seven times. On each circuit he must pause to kiss or touch the southeast corner of the Kaaba, where the Black Stone is located. If the press of the crowd prevents this, then the pilgrim must at least point to the corner with the right hand.

The next ritual commemorates Hagar's search for water for her son Ishmael. The pilgrim must walk quickly seven times across the valley between the two small hills of Safa and Marwa. The hills are about 500 yards apart (ibid., p. 447).

Next on the ritual agenda is the march to Mt. Arafat, some 12 miles east of Mecca. Many spend the night at Mina (the halfway point), and continue the journey before dawn. All pilgrims must arrive at Mt. Arafat on the following morning. Once there the pilgrims are required to "stand before Allah" from noon until sunset. They spend the night in the open. The next morning the pilgrims return to Mina, where the *rajm* (the stoning of the devil) is performed and sheep and camels are sacrificed. Three days of feasting follow.

The pilgrims make a final trip around the Kaaba. The discarding of the seamless garment signals the end of the hajj. The pilgrims may assume the title of *Hajj*, indicating he has made the pilgrimage.

The Sixth Pillar of Islam

There is a Sixth Pillar that will seldom be discussed in a modern college comparative religions class. Considering what happened on September 11, 2001, this would seem inexplicable. It was stated by Muhammed to be the second most important thing in Islam. This Sixth Pillar is *jihad* (Morey, *Jihad*, p. 30). You will hear Muslims try to explain away jihad as a "mere personal striving to overcome sin and become a better servant of Allah." However, this is a secondary meaning only. The primary definition of the word in the major dictionaries and encyclopedias (and among Islamic authorities themselves) is "holy war to spread or defend Islam" (ibid., pp. 3-15).

Jihad can be declared by any recognized Islamic authority and can be used to justify any conceivable atrocity or act of terrorism. Thus, it is not just limited to warfare, as it would be recognized or sanctioned in the West. Jihad includes (but is by no mean limited to) the following: genocide, ethnic cleansing, enslavement of non-Muslims, bombing of public transportation, gang rape of non-Muslim women, burning of churches, the murder of Christian ministers, threats against journalists who insult Islam or its prophet, torture, beheadings, assassinations, the desecration of non-Muslim cemeteries, and the destruction of non-Muslim landmarks (ibid., p. 30). So it may be accurate to refer to Islam as "the religion of peace," but the peace of Islam seems only to be that imposed by any other despotic system—all enemies are liquidated and all dissent is muzzled.

Chapter 5: The God of Islam

I. Allah the Lunar Deity

You will often hear certain Christian pastors, theologians, and others solemnly declare, "Christians, Muslims, and Jews all worship the same God." Nothing could be further from the truth. The god of Islam is not the God of Abraham, Issac, and Jacob. After "the battle of the Trenches" and the bloodless conquest of Mecca, Muhammed suppressed the worship of 359 of the 360 gods worshipped by the pagan Arabs. He retained the worship of the lunar deity who was called Allah (a contraction of al-ilah, i.e. "the god") even in pre-Islamic times (Morey, p. 11). Guillaume tells us that "Allah was known from Christian and Jewish sources as the one god, and there can be no doubt whatever that he was known to the pagan Arabs of Mecca as the supreme being" (p. 7). However, the opposite was actually the case. The pagan Arabs readily accepted Muhammed's "new" god because it was a god with which they were already familiar. Muhammed retained the ancient

Aap' 76-77

custom of pilgrimage to Mecca and worship at the sanctuary of the Moon-god called the Kaaba. This is explicable only if it were not generally understood that lesser gods and goddesses were being suppressed and not the supreme lunar deity. The Black Stone, located in the Kaaba (identified as a meteorite by an English explorer who entered Mecca disguised as an Arab) is honored by Muslim pilgrims with a kiss or by stroking it in the same manner that sacred stones were honored in pre-Islamic times. Obviously, the Black Stone had been the fetish of the Moon-god.

Other evidence that Allah originated as a pagan Moon-god: the crescent moon as the symbol of Islam, beginning and ending the fast month of Ramadan with the crescent moon, use of a 354-day ceremonial lunar calendar, and the fact that pagan Arabs never accused Muhammed of preaching a different Allah than the traditional lunar god they already served (Morey, p.12). As you might recall (Chapter 1), besides Allah, the pre-Islamic Arabs worshipped Allat (the Sun), al-Uzza (the planet Venus), and Manat (Fortune). Allat is merely the feminine form of Allah. Thus, Allat means "The goddess"; Allah means "the god." So Allah was borrowed from the sabaism (worship of heavenly bodies) of the ancient Arabs and not from the God of the Bible. This sabaism was universal among the ancient Arabs. The Kaaba at Mecca was not the only such sanctuary. Several nearly identical structures were located in different parts of Arabia each dedicated to one of the seven planets.

II. Identity of the God of Islam Revealed

However, the Muslims themselves do not actually believe that the God of the Christians and Jews is identical to Allah. They believe the God of the Bible is a wimp, whereas their god is a war god, the god of the sword. When Muslims chant "Allah, akhbar" they are not saying "Allah is great", but "Allah is greatest." They are declaring that Allah is above all other gods, including the God of Christians and Jews. This gives us the true identity of the god of the Muslims. Isaiah's prophecy against the ruler of Babylon is actually referring to Satan, who has been trying to de-throne the Creator since the beginning. This Muslim chant sounds strikingly like Satan's boasts:

"I will ascend into heaven, I will exalt my throne above the stars of God: I will sit also upon the mount of the congregation, in the sides of the north: I will ascend above the heights of the clouds; I will be like the most High" (Isa. 14:13,14).

Chapter 6: Sources of Authority

Quran
Hadith
Ijma
Qiyas

⎯⎯⎯ᘉᘉ⎯⎯⎯

The Quran is Islam's highest source of authority. There are three other sources: (1) The Hadith, (2) Ijma, and (3) Qiyas. Sharia (the totality of Islamic law) can be based on any of these, but is most influenced by the Quran and the Hadith, especially the latter.

I. The Quran

Quran literally means "reading" or "recitation." It is also called *Al-Kitab*, "The Book." A *mashaf* is a handwritten copy of the Quran, often beautifully illuminated (Shorrosh, p. 24). Former Iraqi dictator and the now deceased Saddam Hussein possessed a mashaf written in his own blood.

A person able to memorize and repeat the entire Quran in Arabic is called a *hafiz* ("protector"). Such a person will often just be memorizing mere sounds and will have no idea what they mean, because a hafiz may not even understand the Classical Arabic of the Quran. The blind will sometimes memorize the Quran to receive the title (ibid., pp. 21, 22).

The Quran is divided into 114 suras of 6200 verses and about 80,000 words. In order for the entire book to be read during the month of Ramadan, it is further divided into thirty sections which are called *juz* or *sipara* (ibid., p. 26).

The arrangement of suras is determined by length. The longest suras are placed at the beginning and the shortest are toward the end. The only exception to this is the opening sura, The Fatiha:

> In the name of Allah
> The compassionate and merciful
> Praise Allah, Lord of the worlds
> The compassionate and merciful
> Ruler of the Day of Judgment
> We serve Thee alone
> We call to Thee alone for help
> Lead us in the straight path
> The path of those whom Thou hast blessed
> Not the path of those who incur Thy wrath
> Nor of those who go astray

Internal contradictions in the Quran are resolved by the so-called doctrine of *abrogation*. Certain verses in the Quran are *mansukh*, or annulled by other verses revealed later (ibid., p. 163). (Apparently, Allah had a hard time making up his mind about some matters). This principle is annunciated in the Sura of the Cow (2:106): "Some of Our revelations We abrogate or cause to be forgotten. In their place we bring one superior or of like manner. Dost thou not know that Allah canst do all things?"

The Hadith

The word *hadith* primarily means "communication" or "narrative." It may refer to such that are either sacred or profane. In a technical sense hadith means "The Tradition," i.e., the record of what Muhammed said, did, allowed (*halal*), or forbade (*haram*). The discipline of interpreting and evaluating The Tradition is called *ilm al-hadith* (Gibb and Kramers, p. 116).

An individual command or example given by Muhammed is called a *sunna* (pl. sunan). It means "custom" or "use," but when in reference to the Prophet a "rule" or "statute." Whether a particular sunna is authentic or not depends upon its *isnad* (or *sanad*), i.e., the chain of those who transmitted it. If a sunna can be traced back to a *sahabi* (person who lived in the society of Muhammed), it would generally have greater authority than one only traced back to the *tabiun* (the generation immediately following Muhammed). A sunna going back to the tabiun would be more authoritative than one that could be traced only as far as the *tabiu al-tabiin* (second generation after Muhammed). Of course, the most authoritative of all sunan are those going back to Muhammed himself, generally speaking (ibid.).

Sunna came to mean "standard" in the sense of that which is conventional or orthodox. Thus, a

Sunni is a Muslim who considers himself one who practices the orthodox brand of Islam, as opposed to the "sectarians," i.e., the Shiites.

The Hadith at one time was enormous, containing no less than 600,000 individual sunan. A 9th century scholar by the name of al-Bukhari reduced the number to 7,275 he deduced to be *al-Sahih* ("the genuine"). Abu Daud sifted through 50,000 rules and only accepted 4,800 as genuine. There are other such hadith collections, but none are universally accepted by all Muslims.

In theory, the Hadith is a lesser authority than the Quran. However in practice the Hadith and Quran are equal. According to tradition, "a prohibition by the Prophet of Allah is equal to a prohibition by Allah" (ibid., p. 552).

III. Ijma

According to Sunni jurisprudence, *ijma* is the consensus of those knowledgeable enough to practice *ijtihad* ("independent judicial reasoning"). A *mujtahid* is a title held by a Muslim legal scholar who has attained the highest rank.

Ijma is a source of Islamic jurisprudence or *fiqh*, which is further defined as "the practice of discovering God's law (SHAR'IAH), writing treatises about it, and relating the practice of law to revelation" [*sic*.] (Newby, p. 63).

An analogy has been made between ijma and the High Church doctrine of the *consensus doctorum ecclesiarum*, since deviation from ijma is branded as *bida* ("innovation"). Such an "innovation" would correspond to the ecclesiastical notion of heresy (Guillaume, p. 101).

Four schools (*madhhabs*) of Islamic jurisprudence have developed, each with its own interpretations of the Quran and Hadith (all are considered orthodox by Sunnis): (1) the Malaki, (2) the Hanafi, (3) the Shafii, and (4) the Hanbali. The Shafii and Hanbali are the strictest interpreters of the Quran and Hadith. The Malaki school interprets Islamic law on the basis of the consensus of the *umma*, or the community of the faithful. The Hanbali School uses the principle of analogy to reach legal conclusions.

Each madhhab has its geographical center. The Malaki is dominant in North Africa. The Hanafi is dominant in Turkey. The Hanbali and Shafii schools are based mainly in Egypt and Syria (Nigosian, p. 450). Shiites have their own schools of jurisprudence.

IV. Qiyas

Qiyas is reasoning by analogy. It is the application of a principle which governs legal cases that are more or less parallel. It reduces all Islamic practices to five categories: (1) obligatory, (2) recommended, (3) indifferent, (4) disapproved but not forbidden, and (5) forbidden (ibid.).

The term *fatwa* has become familiar to non-Muslims mainly because it has been associated with declarations of jihad or with pronouncements of death on various authors and publishers who have allegedly insulted Islam. However, traditionally a fatwa is a religiously based legal judgment on issues of daily Islamic life given by a *mufti* (a man learned in the sharia). Fatwas have been collected into manuals and are used as guides in helping to determine the ijma. *Qadis* ("judges") also use fatwas in reaching their decisions.

Conclusion

A student of Islamic law must know the Quran by heart, master the Hadith, and study the earliest extant commentaries. He is then allowed to begin the study of *ilm il-usul* or "the discipline of the fundamental principles"—which is the aggregate of the Quran, Hadith, Ijma, and Qiyas (Shorrosh, p. 23).

This study regimen requires a good memory, but not analytical thinking. It is plain to see that in such a system original thinking would have no place. Shakespeare certainly deserves the title of "The Bard." However, suppose right after his death in the early 17th century the society of that day had determined that since the plays and sonnets of this man were without equal, his writings would now become a kind of canon. All behavior, laws, art, literature, etc., had to conform to a Bardic Standard. If a practice, enterprise, or institution could not be established by some text in the Shakespearian Corpus or by something Shakespeare commanded, did, allowed, or prohibited, it would be declared heretical by the Keepers of the Bardic Standard. Stratford-on-Avon would certainly have been made into a holy place, but more importantly, material and social progress would have been arrested. This illustrates what has happened in much of the Islamic world.

Chapter 7: The Sects of Islam

———⟨⟩⟨⟩———

Introduction

The body of Muhammed was hardly cold in the grave when Islam was rent by its first divisions (see Ch. 3). Supposedly, he even predicted that Islam would eventually be divided into 73 sects, and that they would all be heretical except the one sect professed by him and his companions. There are now more than 150 Islamic sects, more than double the number of Muhammed's prophecy (Shorrosh, p. 35). Hence, only some of the most important of these sects can be discussed.

I. Kharijites

The origin of these "seceders" represented a kind of "third way" in the Hashemite/Ommaiyid dispute that eventually divided Islam into its present-day Sunni and Shiite branches. The Kharijites were

K Kharijites

radical egalitarians who believed Muhammed's successor ought to be elected by the free-choice of the entire umma.

All Muslims are concerned about ritual purity before praying. The Kharijites were even more concerned about moral purity. According to them, an unrepentant sinner was no better than an infidel. They felt the same way about unjust rulers and those who refused to fight against them.

Today the Kharijites are known as *Abadis*. They can be found in North Africa, Oman, and Zanzibar. They form a separate community outside of the four Sunni madhhabs. Kharijitism's greatest legacy is the undoubted influence it has had on Wahhabism (Guillaume, pp. 112-114).

II. Sunnis

orthodox

The vast majority of Muslims (80-85%) are Sunnis. They acknowledge as Muhammed's rightful successor the first four caliphs (Abu Bakr, Omar, Othman, and Ali). According to Sunnis, Muhammed's line of succession to the caliphate is not limited to Muhammed's family, but includes the entire Quraysh tribe. Sunnis also maintain that Islam's only authoritative basis rests on the Quran, as interpreted by the sunna (tradition) and the ijma (consensus). On these two fundamental issues Sunnis and Shiites differ (Nigosian, p. 451).

III. Shiites

sectarious

Sunnis call Shiites "the Rafidi," or "those who forsake the truth." However, the Shiites refer to themselves as *al-Muminun* ("the true believers"). They maintain that Muhammed personally designated his cousin Ali to be the leader of the Islamic community following his death. Shiites also elevated into an additional "pillar of Islam" the notion that the faithful must believe in all the Imams, especially the Imam revealed for their own age. The Imam is made infallible by means of a special gift from Allah. He alone can rightly interpret the Quran. It is popularly believed that on a sunny day the Imam casts no shadow and that he is supernaturally protected from physical harm. Some Shiites are even convinced that Ali and the Imams are incarnations of the Godhead (Guillaume, p. 118).

Imamites or "Twelvers"

Shiitism was very soon beset by divisions. The largest and most important of these are the followers of the Twelfth Imam, also known as "Twelvers" or Imamites. They acknowledge the Twelve Imams descended from Ali through his wife Fatima (another daughter of Muhammed). The line ends with Muhammed al-Mahdi, who simply disappeared one day in the year 880. He is believed to be "the hidden Imam" who will return one day as the Mahdi ("guided one"), who will restore true Islam and bring righteousness to the world.

Ismailis

Another Shiite group is known as the Ismailis.
They regard a little-known man by the name of
Ismail as the seventh Imam. (Sunnis and Twelvers
say that he was an evil man who was not allowed to
succeed to the office of Imam by his father Jafar).
Since Ismailism has become a secret society, its core
of inner teachings is known only to initiates.

Ismailism has given the English language the
word "assassin." The word is a corruption of *hashishin*. The Hashishin were members of an Ismaili sect
who were sent out to murder their master's opponents
while intoxicated on hashish, a potent derivative of
the marijuana plant (ibid., pp. 122, 123).

The Druzes

The Druzes get their name from one al-Darazi.
He proclaimed the divinity of the Fatimid Caliph in
Cairo, known as al-Hakim bi-Amrillah (reigned 996-
1021 A.D.). Al-Darazi later settled in Syria where
he was probably murdered in 1019 A.D. In 1021
al-Hakim departed on a trip from which he never
returned. Whether he was also murdered or just
disappeared is impossible to say. Two other Druze
figures are Hamazah ibn Ali and Baha al-Din. In 1043
these two left Egypt with some others to an unknown
destination and were never heard from again. The
Druzes believe al-Hakim is still alive in concealment
and that Hamzah and Baha will return on the Day of

Judgment. Since that year Druzism has been closed to new converts.

Druzes believe in the oneness of Allah, the teachings of intermediaries (including Adam, Moses, Jesus, and Muhammed), and in the transmigration of souls. Druzist authority rests on Biblical and Quranic texts, as well as on the *Hikmah*, a body of esoteric literature concerning theology, cosmology, and eschatology (Encycl. of Rel., pp. 2501-2504).

IV. Wahhabism

The Wahhabist sect was founded by Muhammed ibn Abd al-Wahhab. He railed against what he saw as the apostate condition of Islam in 18th century Arabia. He gathered together a group of disciples and in 1744 he made an alliance with Muhammed ibn Saud, who ruled the small oasis town of Daraiya in central Arabia. This alliance was based on the teachings of ibn Taimiiya, a medieval reformer who believed the perfect Islamic society would be composed of two classes of authority: the *ulama*, who know sharia; and the *umara*, who wield the political power necessary to enforce it. The alliance between ibn Saud and al-Wahhab became the basis upon which the modern state of Saudi Arabia was established almost two centuries later (Cole, pp. 117-119).

V. Sufis

Sufism is synonymous with Islamic mysticism. The meaning of the term *Sufi* is disputed, but it probably comes from the Arabic word *suf* ("wool"), signifying the rough woolen garments worn by early Sufi *darwishes* (members of a Sufi fraternity).

Sufism originally arose as a reaction against the excessive scholasticism, legalism, and ritualism of medieval Islam. That Eastern mysticism has greatly influenced the movement cannot be denied. The Sufi *shaikh* or *pir* (master) is very much like a Hindu guru in that his followers owe him absolute obedience and veneration. The transmigration of souls is accepted. Meditation and asceticism are principal forms of religious expression, and some Sufi groups practice ritual self-mutilation. Other Eastern ideas adopted by Sufis include the concepts of the "third eye," absorption of the individual will into that of the divine, and a de-emphasis on the dichotomy between good and evil. Techniques of inducing autohypnosis through repetitive chanting (called *dhiker*) and controlled breathing also reveal an Eastern influence.

Sufi orders or fraternities are centered around their founders. Their graves serve as pilgrimage sites for the fraternity's darwishes. The *tekke* or *zawiyah* (Sufi monastery) has become the center of public worship, often taking the place of the mosque (Nigosian, p. 453).

VI. Bahais

Shiites often refer to the twelve legitimate imams as *babs* ("gates"), since they are gates through which the faithful gain access to the truth. The mysterious disappearance of the Twelfth Imam has fueled the belief he would someday reappear as the Mahdi. In 1844 a Persian Shiite named Ali Muhammed declared himself to be the Twelfth Imam and began to call himself the Bab. He started a reform movement that soon gained so many followers that the authorities reacted by executing the Bab on July 9, 1850. The movement was suppressed. However, before his death the Bab predicted a great leader would arise who would complete his work of establishing the universal religion based upon brotherhood and love (ibid., p. 460).

Mirza Hussain Ali took over the leadership of the remnants of the movement. He assumed the title Bahaullah ("Allah's glory"). In 1853 he was exiled to Baghdad. Ten years later the authorities exiled him again, this time to Istanbul. Just before he departed he announced to his followers he was the leader whose coming had been foretold by the Bab. Eventually, Bahaullah was sent to a prison colony at Acre, Palestine. From 1868 until his death in 1892 he continued to advocate the unification of Judaism, Christianity, and Muhammedanism through his teaching and writings, which comprise 100 volumes (Shorrosh, p. 38, 39). Other important Bahai leaders are Abdul Baha (1844-1921), Bahaullah's eldest son, and Shogi Effendi (1896-1957), Abdul's grandson.

Bahais believe God is unknowable but reveals himself, in part, through messengers they call "manifestations of God." These include Abraham, Moses, Zoroaster, Krishna, Buddha, Jesus, Muhammed, and Bahaullah. Bahais also believe in charity, equality of the sexes, peace, world government, human rights, the Golden Rule, and a universal language. The world headquarters of the sect is in Haifa, Israel (Nigosian, pp. 462-465).

VII. Ahmadiya

This sect was founded by Mirza Ghulam Ahmad al-Qadiani who died in 1908. A series of visions convinced him he was the Mahdi. By 1889 he had gathered around him his first discipiles. The movement grew rapidly both before and after his death. In 1914 the movement split into the Qadianis and the Lahoris (after Lahore, Pakistan; at the time part of British India). The Lahoris insist on defending a modern, progressive Islam, whereas the Qadianis emphasize the uniqueness of the founder as a prophet.

The writings of al-Qadiani are voluminous. They are a strange mixture of conservative and reformist ideas. For example, he condemned jihadism and any coercion in religion, yet upheld the institutions of polygyny and *purdah* (the seclusion of women).

The most controversial teaching of al-Qadiani was the identification of himself as prophet *after* Muhammed, contradicting the orthodox position that Muhammed was "the seal of the prophets," i.e., the final messenger of Allah. The ulama condemned al-Qadiani's claim of prophethood, and his followers have become a persecuted minority in Pakistan. Many Ahmadis moved from India to Pakistan since 1947, only to become a target of one hate campaign after another (1949, 1952, 1953, and 1974). Finally, in 1974 the Pakistani constitution was amended so that Ahmadis were declared a non-Muslim minority. The amendment barred Ahmadis from holding public office in that nation (<u>Abingdon Dict.</u>, pp. 16, 17).

Chapter 8: Muslim False Arguments, Assertions, and Outright Lies Exposed

_____ ᘓᓑ᠂ᓚ_____

The Quran is letter for letter what was given to the Prophet Muhammed.

Answer: Before they were gathered and edited by Zeyd (Muhammed's amanuensis or secretary), the words of Muhammed existed as a haphazard collection hastily copied on stones, palm leaves, and even on the bones of animals. Many other sayings could be found only in the recollections of his followers. During the War of The Apostasy, occurring right after the Prophet's death, so many of the *ashab* ("Companions of the Prophet") were killed in a battle at the oasis known as The Garden of Death, that many of Muhammed's saying were in danger of being lost. Zeyd wrote down as much of this material as he could from the recollections of the surviving Companions. He gave the entire collection to Abu Bakr, the first caliph. This collection was bequeathed to Hafsa, Abu Bakr's daughter and a widow of Muhammed. From this collection four different versions of the Quran circulated. Under Caliph Othman, a commission was formed (in which Zeyd would play a leading part), and they issued an "authorized" edition and Othman commanded that all Muslims must accept it. However, the *ulama* (religious authorities) in the city of Kufa (now a ruin in present-day Iraq) refused this version and continued to use one of their own. Copies of this version could still be found until the 10th century.

Even today scholars cannot agree on the Quranic text. Variant readings exist for both vowels and for the more important consonants. Islamic scholars have ducked this issue by simply declaring all variant readings as having equal authority. So apparently the Quran as it now exists couldn't possibly have been letter for letter what was originally given to Muhammed.

Only a miracle can account for the Quran since Muhammed was illiterate.

Answer: Muhammed was *not* illiterate. He was commanded by the angel Gabriel to "recite" in his initial revelation while spending the night at Mt. Hira near Mecca. The word "recite" (from which the word "Quran" comes from) means to "read." Also, he personally signed the Treaty of Hudaybiya with the Quraysh. Again, while on his deathbed, he asked his wife Ayisha for writing material to record the name of his successor (he was too weak to do so). Furthermore, the monks at St. Catherine's monastery at the foot of Jebel Musa (Mt. Sinai) can produce a letter from the hand of Muhammed himself granting the monastery protection in perpetuity. This does not exhaust the evidence for his literacy, either. Since Muhammed was obviously literate, we can "write" off this Muslim supernatural claim, as well.

Since Muhammed was illiterate and the Quran is grammatically perfect, only a supernatural act can account for that.

Answer: The first part of this claim we have just dealt with. The fact is the Quran contains a number of grammatical faux pas. These are listed by Dr. Ani Shorrosh in his book Islam Revealed in the following *suras* or chapters of the Quran: (1) 2:177 (The Cow), (2) 7:160 (The Heights), (3) 4:162 (The Women), (4) 5:69 (The Table Spread), (5) 63:10 (The Hypocrites), (6) 3:59 (The Family of Imran). We should not expect to find many errors in the Quran, considering the editing that was done initially by Zeyd and later by the commission assembled by Caliph Othman. So this alleged "miracle" also falls flat.

Since the Quran is the most perfect specimen of literature ever written, it must be the word of Allah.

Answer: Anyone who has attempted to read through an English translation of the Quran would have to disagree vehemently. Thomas Carlyle has stated that only a sense of duty could carry a European through the task of reading it. Great literature will come through even in translation. Anyone who has read the Bible, Homer, Virgil, or Tolstoy in translation would agree. The Quran is surely an important document, but it hardly deserves to be called a literary masterpiece. It is a disjointed and disorganized tangle with barely a single topic thoroughly discussed in any single sura (of which there are 114). Certainly, an all-powerful Allah would have sent down his "perfected" revelation to humanity in a perfectly organized manner? In the Middle East professional reciters of the Quran sing-song passages from out of it in Arabic beautifully, but it cannot stand by itself as great literature.

The Bible has been so completely corrupted that it has been lost.

Answer: This assertion does not stand up to the evidence any better than the other Muslim assertions we have investigated. There is no text of literature from the ancient world better attested to than the text of the Bible. This is true of both the Old and New Testaments. The oldest texts of the Old Testament are the Samaritan Pentateuch (5th cen. B.C.) and the Septuagint (3rd cen. B.C.). These are substantially the same as the Massoretic Text from the 10th cen. A.D. The Old Testament text of the Latin Vulgate translated by Jerome from Hebrew manuscripts early in the 5th cen. A.D. also shows no substantial difference from the three other textual traditions. The text of the New Testament can be reconstructed from over 20,000 ancient manuscripts. Scholars deem the present content of modern editions of the Greek New Testament to be within about 99.5% of the autographs. The autographs are the original documents as they would have been penned by the apostolic authors.

All of the different Bible translations prove it is corrupt.

Answer: This argument ignores the fact that the Quran itself has been translated into dozens of different languages. There are over 50 English translations of the Quran alone. The various Bible translations are all different because there are so many different ways to express one's self in any language. A simple statement in English like, "I'm going to the store" can be said any number of ways: "I'm going to the market","I'm going shopping", "I think I'll do some horse-trading", "I need some things at the store", etc., all express the same idea. Similarly, when expressing words and concepts from one language into another, there are any numbers of ways to do so.

There exist different methods or philosophies of translation, as well. There is the *interlinear* method which translates a text word-for-word in the same order the words are found in the original. This is hardly a translation at all since the interlinear method still renders a good deal of the original text unintelligible to a reader unfamiliar with it. There is the *literal* method of translation which attempts to convey the exact meaning of the words of the original text in a manner that makes it understandable to the reader. Translators using this method will usually not try to clean up obscure portions of the original text but render them as they stand. The *dynamic-equivalency* method expresses the idea in the original text with an equivalent idea in another language. Translators using this method will attempt to make obscure passages in the original intelligible in translation. Then there is the *paraphrase*, a very free translation often rendered in a colloquial dialect. All of these methods have been used in translating the Bible and no translation using any of them is "wrong" as long as it faithfully renders the original. This in no way indicates textual corruption. Hence, this Muslim argument is no better thought out than any of the others.

Since there are so many Christian denominations, that must indicate Christianity is not well thought out.

Answer: What is not well thought out is this argument since it conveniently ignores the fact that Islam was beset with divisions almost before the corpse of Muhammed could grow cold in the ground. A council chose Abu Bakr as Muhammed's successor ("caliph"). Immediately, a number of tribes declared their independence from the *umma* (i.e., the Muslim community). Some even chose leaders of their own to be the "seal of the prophets." This schism was put down with much blood and fire (*The War of the Apostasy*, discussed earlier). The election of Ali to the caliphate permanently divided Islam into the Sunni and Shiite branches. The Kharijites, also known as Abadis, can be found today in North Africa, Oman, and Zanzibar. They form a separate community outside of the four Sunni madhhabs (i.e., schools of jurisprudence). Today there are some 150 different sects of Islam with more forming all the time.

There are many different denominations of Christianity because in most countries of the Western world people have the liberty to freely associate. We also have a thing unknown in almost all Muslim countries—freedom of religion or even from religion according to the dictates of the individual conscience. In Muslim countries, even if this liberty might exist on paper, it does not actually exist in fact. Families, employers, friends, and religious authorities will keep a person from belonging to a religion of his or her own choice. To convert to another religion more often than not places a person in jeopardy for their very life. They may be subject to arrest and imprisonment. At the very least, such a person could expect the loss of employment and social ostracism. There is usually a state-supported version of Islam and the religious authorities have a great deal of influence through however much of the *sharia* (canon law) that country accepts as part of its legal structure.

Unlike Christianity, Islam is free of racial prejudice.

Answer: This assertion also conveniently turns a blind eye even to recent history. However, in the 16th century a vicious campaign was conducted by the Sunni Turks which virtually eliminated all

Persian Shiites in Anatolia. Arab Muslims suffered greatly under the rule of their Turkish co-religionists. In recent times, the predominantly Moorish military and police of the Islamic Republic of Mauritania routinely harass, kill, and attempt to drive away Senegalese settlers in the southern part of the country, even though these settlers are also Muslims (Langewiesche, pp. 257, 258). In the Sudan non-Arab Muslims in the south are also targets of government extermination along with Christians and animists. Sunni Arabs in Iraq conducted a war of extermination for several decades against Muslim Kurds in the northern mountains. Theoretically Islam, as does Christianity, accepts all races into a single brotherhood. In practice, Muslims have done no better at living up to their ideals than Christians, but to this day still conduct wars of genocide even against those who share the same religious faith.

Since Jesus was not actually crucified, he cannot be an atonement for sin.

Answer: According to sura 4:155: "They did not kill him and they did not crucify him, but one was made to resemble him." Although this sura is contradicted by others that *do* indicate Jesus' death on the cross, Muslims almost universally deny the crucifixion of Jesus. Since Islam is preeminently a religion based upon works-righteousness, the fact that Jesus was nailed to a cross in order to become a sacrifice for sin would have no importance whatever for its adherents.

The phrase "one was made to resemble him" comes from an old idea that circulated among the Jews that Jesus was some kind of sorcerer who could cast his form upon another or could change his form into someone else. Even Christian heretics in Muhammed's day held to such notions. This is an indication of Jewish folklore and pseudo-Christian influences upon the contents of the Quran and casts further doubt upon its divine origin.

That a man by the name of Yeshua bar Yoseph was executed by the Romans at the instigation of the Jewish religious leaders is one of the best documented facts from the ancient world. It is mentioned in apostolic, patristic, rabbinic, and secular sources. You can read about eyewitness accounts of His death in the New Testament (Mt. 27; Mk.15; Lk. 23; Jn. 19; I Pet. 2:23-24). Clement of Rome, who lived at the end of the Apostolic Age and who was probably an associate of some of these eyewitnesses, wrote of it. Polycarpus, a disciple of John (who was present at the crucifixion) also tells us that Jesus died upon the cross. Josephus mentions His death in the *Testimonium Flavianum*, a passage hotly disputed in times past but now generally viewed by Christian and Jewish scholars to be authentic (with a few possible interpolations). Tacitus mentions the death of Jesus as does Pliny the Younger. The Jewish Talmud mentions Him as a practitioner of black magic who was justly condemned to death. Additionally, the Old Testament is replete with prophecies concerning His death (Gen. 3:15; Ps. 22; Isa. 53; Zech. 12:10).

Again, we find the teachings of Islam playing fast and loose with the facts of history.

Since Abraham was the first Muslim, Islam was prior to both Judaism and Christianity.

Answer: Muhammed used the good name of Abraham to assert the primacy of Islam over both Judaism and Christianity. He claimed the patriarch was a Muslim. Indeed, it was Abraham's submission to the ultimate test of offering his son in sacrifice (described in the Quran by the verb *aslama*) that likely gave the religion of Islam its name). However, the Quran incorrectly identifies the son as Ishmael. The Bible correctly informs us Abraham "bound *Isaac* (italics mine) his son, and laid him on the altar...and took the knife to slay his son" (Gen. 22:10,11). Also, in order to hallow a heathen sanctuary in Mecca (the Kaaba) and make it fit for Muslim use, Muhammed made up a story out of whole cloth that Abraham and Ishmael visited the place and originally reared up that sanctuary. An ancient heathen rite—the pilgrimage to Mecca—became a pillar of Islam by another stroke of Muhammed's revisionism.

According to the Quran (sura 2:25), Abraham initiated the pilgrimage there. However, there is absolutely no historical evidence whatever to assert that either Abraham or Ishmael ever visited Mecca. In fact, with the possible exception of the queen of Sheba (see II Chron. 9:1-13), no biblical figure ever traveled to that city. Travelers heading north from Sheba would have certainly refreshed themselves at

Mecca's famed well of Zamzam. However, the wise and beautiful monarch could have traveled to Israel by ship and transferred her gifts for Solomon onto a caravan at Eloth, Israel's southern port. After all, she ruled over a people who were also accomplished mariners.

Jesus never claimed to be divine.

Answer: When Jesus walked upon the waters of the Sea of Galilee (Mt. 14:22-33; Mk. 6:45-52), His disciples saw Him from their boat and cried out in fear. They believed they had seen a ghost. Most English translations cover up Jesus' response. For example, the King James Version says, "Be of good cheer: it is I: be not afraid" (Mk. 6:50). However, the Greek literally translated says, "Fear not, I am." This is exactly the term He used in John 8:58 when He referred to Himself with the divine name *I Am* (*ego eimi*). This was also how God revealed Himself to Moses at the burning bush in Exodus 3:14 in the Septuagint (*Ego eimi ho on*). Jesus' adversaries certainly understood these words to be a divine claim, since they were prepared to stone Him for blasphemy (Jn. 8:59).

This was not the first attempt on Jesus' life prompted by His claim to deity. After healing a lame man on the Sabbath, the religious authorities condemned Him. Jesus' answer—"My Father worketh hitherto, and I work" (Jn. 5:17)—aroused their ire even more. Not only had He profaned the

Sabbath, "but said also that God was his Father, making himself equal with God" (vs. 18).

Jesus also claimed for Himself the authority to forgive sins (Mk. 2:5-7). The Bible clearly teaches this is something that only God can do (Isa. 43:25).

Jesus applied terms to Himself that are only explicable if He were making claims to divinity: "I am the resurrection, and the life" (Jn. 11:25); "He that believeth on me, believeth not on me, but on him that sent me" (Jn. 12:44); "I am the way, the truth, and the life" (Jn. 14:6); "he that hath seen me hath seen the Father" (Jn. 14:9), etc.

Jesus also called Himself "the Son of God." The term is not a mere title, nor is it the declaration of a mystic's attainment of his personal union with divinity. As used by Jesus, the term expresses His equality with God. God Himself authenticated Jesus' unique Sonship by His resurrection from the dead (Rom. 1:4).

However, the most common title Jesus used in the Synoptic Gospels is "Son of Man." Formerly, expositors were inclined to see in this term the Lord Jesus identifying Himself with frail mortals. More than likely, "Son of Man" refers to the following passage in the Book of Daniel (7:13, 14):

"I saw in the night visions, and behold, one like the Son of Man came with the clouds of heaven, and came to the Ancient of days, and they brought him near before him. And there was given him dominion, and glory, and a kingdom, that all people, nations, and languages, should serve him: his dominion is an everlasting dominion, which shall not pass away, and his kingdom that which shall not be destroyed."

Thus, far from indicating mere humanity, the term is applicable to a Being of great power and glory. William Lane Craig observes:

"The Son of Man was a divine figure in the Old Testament book of Daniel who would come at the end of the world to judge mankind and rule forever. Thus, the claim to be the Son of Man would be in effect a claim to divinity" (The Son Rises: Historical Evidence for the Resurrection of Jesus, p. 140; quoted by Stroble, p. 37).

So the statement accepted by the Council of Nicea (325 A.D.) that "Jesus Christ is very God of very God, of one substance with the Father and begotten of the Father from eternity" was not an invention of the attending bishops (Qualben, p. 122). The deity of Christ was part of the belief system of the church from its very beginning, because it originated with the Lord Jesus Christ Himself.

The doctrine of the Trinity is found in only one Bible verse (I John 5:7), and the important part of that verse is a late textual gloss not found in the original manuscript.

Answer: The better manuscripts of I Jn. 5:7 read: "For there are three that bear record." The rest of the verse—"in heaven, the Father, the Word, and the Holy Ghost: and these three are one," and the first clause of verse 8 are, indeed, spurious. No Greek manuscript prior to the 16th century contains these words. Nonetheless, at the Council of Nicea (325 A.D.), Athanasius prevailed upon the assembled bishops to accept a statement concerning the relationship between the Father and the Son which has since been recognized as Christian orthodoxy, to wit: (1) the Son is eternally generated from the Father, (2) the Son is of the same nature (*homousia*), and (3) while there is no division or separation in God's essential being, the Father and the Son remain distinct Persons.

The Council of Alexandria (362 A.D.) accepted the proposition that the Holy Spirit is not created, but is of the same substance, and is inescapable from the Father and the Son. Obviously, the doctrine of the Trinity is based on proof texts other than the textual gloss in question, since it is not found in *any* authority until late in the 5th century A.D., over a century after the ecumenical councils mentioned above!

Modern-day Palestinians are the direct descendants of the original Canaanite inhabitants of the land.

Answer: There is only one reason the Palestinians would make such an absurd claim, and that is to assert they are not only entitled to the Gaza Strip and the West Bank, but the entire modern State of Israel.

The Canaanites were an ancient people who spoke Ugaritic, a language similar to Hebrew. The ancient land of Canaan was roughly conterminous with the modern State of Israel. About 1451 B.C. the Israelites invaded Canaan. They killed, drove out, or enslaved most of the native population, although many retained their independence (Josh. 6:1-12:24; Judg. 1:1-3:7). Over time the Canaanites merged with either the Israelites or their pagan neighbors through intermarriage or acculturation. In any case, they disappeared from history in ancient times.

In an interview with the Dutch newspaper <u>Dagblad de Verdieping Trouw</u> (Mar. 31, 1977), PLO executive committee member Zahir Mushein admitted, "In reality today there is no difference between Jordanians, Palestinians, Syrians, and Lebanese" (Meir-Levi, pp. 37, 38).

God only gave Israel the land temporarily.

Answer: God promised to give the land of Canaan to Abraham and to his progeny in perpetuity (Gen. 13:15; 15:18). However, that the covenant was not intended to include *all* of Abraham's descendants is evident:

And God said, Sarah thy wife shall bear thee a son indeed: and thou shalt call his name Isaac: and I will establish my covenant with him for an everlasting covenant and with his seed after him (Gen. 17:19).

The covenant was further restricted to Jacob and his descendants ((Gen. 28:13). God later changed Jacob's name to Israel at Peniel (Gen. 32:28). This new name would later be applied to both the nation and the land they would occupy.

A cursory reading of Scripture might give one the impression that the covenant was conditional and based entirely upon the obedience of its recipients

(Lev. 26:33). However, the covenant is reiterated in Scripture (II Ki. 13:23; I Chron. 16:15-18; Acts 7:8; Rom. 4:13). The following passage in the Psalms (105:8-11) represents them all:

"He hath remembered his covenant for ever, the word which he commanded to a thousand generations. Which covenant he made with Abraham, and his oath unto Isaac; and confirmed the same unto Jacob for a law, and to Israel for an everlasting covenant: Saying, Unto thee will I give the land of Canaan, the lot of your inheritance."

It would seem the people of Israel have permanent title to the land known in ancient times as Canaan. Whether they occupy it or not makes no difference, God will providentially arrange for their return no matter how long they have been away from it.

Chapter 9: Islam and Terror

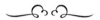

Introduction

Terrorism is political violence that targets civilian or high-profile, symbolic landmarks. Terrorists seek out such "soft" targets because they often lack the expertise to attack "hard" targets such as military installations. Attacking such soft targets can become an end in itself. Nothing advertises the real or imagined grievances of a terrorist group like a bombing that provides a high body count or the destruction of some structure with great symbolic value. How terrorism became the principal tool of radical Islam is a rather complicated story.

I. The Fedayeen and the PLO

The first Arab-Israeli War actually began months before the regular armies of Egypt, Jordan, Iraq, Syria, and Lebanon attacked following Israel's declaration of independence on May 14, 1948. Fighting was already taking place between Jewish settlers and Arab irregulars. One group of about five or six thousand under Abdul Kadar was called the Army of the Jihad. Kadar was a nephew of the notorious pro-Nazi Grand Mufti of Jerusalem, the Haj Amin al Husseini. Self-styled "Field Marshall" Fawzi Kaukji led the Arab Army of Liberation, a mixed force of about 8,000 Arabs, Bosnians, Pakistanis, and African Muslims. Kaukji's army also contained sizable numbers of former members of the Waffen SS, British Army deserters, and ex-members of Mussolini's Blackshirt formations. The Muslim Brotherhood (*Ikhwan al-Muslimin*) was a guerrilla group of about one thousand backed by Egypt. Other smaller irregular Arab forces also operated during this phase of the war. However, none of these groups had much stomach for actual fighting. They distinguished themselves mainly against unarmed civilians, both Arab and Jewish.

Operations against civilian targets would characterize the *fedayeen* activity that would continue against Israel even after the ceasefire that ended the First Arab-Israeli War in February of 1949.

The word *fedayeen* means "self-sacrifice," but there was nothing altruistic about the terror operations conducted by the fedayeen from 1949 until the Second Arab-Israeli War of 1956. There were 2494 armed incidents by Arab infiltrators into Israel during those years. Over one thousand civilians were killed and wounded. There was not a single case of a fedayeen attack on a strictly military target. Fedayeen "fighters" received regular pay, but documents captured by the Israelis revealed the supplementary payment of bonuses for each proven atrocity:

"...it is now known that the sort of proof offered by the fedayeen included trophies such as an ear or finger cut from a corpse, a child's blood-stained copybook, or a family photograph spattered with blood" (Henriques, pp., 194, 195).

After the creation of the Palestine Liberation Organization (PLO) in 1964 many of the fedayeen irregulars were incorporated into that organization's military arm. Incidentally, the "Palestine" this terrorist organization originally sought to liberate was not the Gaza Strip or the West Bank, but was only the territory made up of the State of Israel at the time (Meir-Levi, p. 36). The PLO was driven out of the Jordanian-controlled West Bank and into Jordan proper following Israel's stunning victory during the 1967 Six-Day War (the Third Arab-Israeli War).

Fedayeen-like raids into Israel and the territories occupied by her continued under the aegis of the PLO. However, the PLO became almost a state-within-a-state such that King Hussein of Jordan lost control both of the organization and much of his country. The PLO high jacked international airliners and forced them to land in the Jordanian desert. Deadly terrorist raids by the PLO into Israeli territory finally forced the Jordanian king's hand. The Jordanian army cracked down in September of 1970. Thousands of Palestinian guerrillas were killed and the survivors were driven into Syria and Lebanon (Spencer, p. 61).

Over the years the PLO began to rely more and more on terror as an instrument of policy while increasingly embracing radical jihadist ideology. In fact, Yasser Arafat laid out a series of strategies in a cell phone speech to a Lebanese radio station that would culminate in a final terrorist jihad that would destroy Israel (Meir-Levi, pp. 54, 55). Obviously, the old gangster never intended to negotiate with Israel in good faith. The Oslo Agreement was only one in a series of maneuvers he hoped would end with the demise of the Jewish state.

II. Support of Terror by Radical Muslim States

Originally, terrorism was the instrument of communists, anarchists, and extreme nationalists. The invention of dynamite in the mid-19th century gave the destructive power of artillery to small groups of individuals who before this would have been nothing more than insignificant malcontents. Terrorism would become a tradition of the radical left so that post-revolution communist states continued to sponsor various terrorist groups throughout much of the 20th century. The Soviet Union, East Germany, Cuba, North Korea, and other communist governments trained, harbored, and equipped international terrorists, including key members of the PLO, the Baader-Meinhoff group, the Italian Red Brigades, etc. Since the fall of the Soviet Union in 1991, terrorism lost its chief benefactor. Since then terrorism of the extreme left has been largely replaced by that of radical Islam.

By 1996 only two communist nations were left that supported terrorism—North Korea and Cuba (lately, neither nation has been particularly active in this kind of activity). At the time the United States government classified five other nations as terrorist sponsors: Iran, Iraq, Syria, Libya, and Sudan. All five are Muslim nations. One writer associates only two of these states (Iran and Sudan) with radical Islam (Huntington, p. 216). Actually, the term "radical" or "fundamentalist" Islam is little more than a quibble. All of the nations in question are "fundamentalist," i.e., founded upon Islamic law and precepts. As we have seen, nearly every Muslim, at least in principle, accepts Islamic teachings concerning jihad. Certain Western political, academic, and religious leaders are fond of referring to Islam as "the religion of peace" and of the bad guys who engage in terror as "high jacking a great religion." However, a sizable proportion of Muslims, perhaps even the vast majority, do not view the jihadists as the bad guys. They are actually folk heroes throughout the Islamic world, although their image has been somewhat tarnished of late in the Mid-East. This is because the terrorist jihadists have now largely targeted fellow Muslims.

Libya definitely falls into the category of "fundamentalist Islamic state." The country's ruler, Colonel Muammar Qaddafi, is a Muslim religious zealot. He advocates a revolutionary, pan-Saharan socialism drawn not from the pages of Das Kapital or The Communist Manifesto, but from the Quran and the Hadith. Like Chairman Mao of Communist China, he has issued his little book of his revolutionary sayings for his followers' edification called the Green Book (green being the color of Islam as red is that of Marxism).

Qaddafi's grandiose scheme to create a unified Islamic Saharan empire (with him as its "Caesar," of course) has gone nowhere. For one thing, his military, which looked strong on paper, proved to be incompetent in battle. His military intervention into Chad in 1982 ended in failure. His army had been badly mauled the year before in a short border war with Egypt. Deposed Ugandan dictator Idi Amin even referred to Libyan troops unsuccessfully sent by Qaddafi to keep him in power as "a bunch of women" (Lawson, p. 98). Although awash in oil cash, which continues to pile up in Swiss bank accounts, the Libyan people get little from their government but empty promises and anti-American rants (Hamza, p. 312).

Qaddafi was a major player in international terrorism. He provided weapons and training to both leftwing (the Provisional IRA and Red Brigades) and Islamic terror groups (the Moro Abu Sayyif and the PLO). His agents were involved in assassinations and airport bombings. Terror attacks on American and British citizens in Europe and the Middle East led to American bombing raids on Libya in mid-April of 1986. Thereafter, Qaddafi seems to have gotten directly out of the terror business (though, doubtless, he is still involved in a smaller, more clandestine way). He continued to develop a nuclear bomb, however. But following the overthrow of Saddam Hussein by the United States and its allies in March of

2003, Qaddafi thought it prudent to abandon entirely his nation's nuclear weapons program.

Even more so than Libya, the Baathist regimes of Syria and Iraq have been seen as "secular." However, anyone with even a cursory knowledge of the history of the Baathist Party would disagree.

The Baath, or Arab Socialist Resistance Party is like Qaddafism in that its pan-Arab nationalism and socialist agendas are based on an ideological synthesis of Islam and communism. The goal of the Baath Party is the establishment of a single Arab state from the Tigris to the Atlantic and the transformation of this state's society by means of an *inkilab* ("revolution," or "overturning"). (This sounds suspiciously like the *khalifa* and *jihad* of the militant Islamists).

Baathism was first conceived by Michael Aflaq, a Syrian Greek Orthodox school teacher who became a communist while studying at the Sorbonne in Paris. Aflaq seems to have converted to Islam. He saw no conflict with this religion and with the secular ideology of communism. In 1953 Aflaq and Salah Bitar (a Sunni) joined forces with the organizer of the pro-peasent Arab Socialist Party, Akram Hourani. The Baath Party was the result of this merger.

The merger of communism and Islam greatly appealed to Arabs everywhere, since the sharing of wealth and natural resources seems to fit with the primitive practices of Islam's founder. The Baath Party borrowed from the communists a tight, clandestine organization with separate units or "cells" whose members are unknown to each other (Spencer, pp. 70, 71). Terrorist groups, such as Al Qaeda, have adopted the same kind of cell organization.

In 1963 the Baath Party came to power in Syria. After power struggles between Baathist leaders, General Hafez al-Assad took over the government after a 1970 coup. He was elected president in 1971 in the kind of "election" we have come to expect in totalitarian regimes. His son Bashar became president following the death of General Assad in 2000.

The Assad family are Alawi Shiites. This explains Syria's good relations with the Shiite mullahs who run Iran. Consequently, the Iranian sponsored terror group known as Hizbollah is able to openly operate against Israel from Syrian-occupied Lebanon. Syria also supports Hamas and the Islamic Jihad terrorist groups.

The Baathists came to power in Iraq in 1968. Saddam Hussein became president of the country in 1979 after rising to the top of the Baath Party. Saddam's background would influence the way he would rule the country. He came from a particularly violent part of north-central Iraq beset by crime and intrigue (Hamza, p. 41). So assassination and terrorism would be particularly suited to Saddam the President as instruments of policy.

Saddam supported terrorism against Israel and the West. The families of Palestinian suicide bombers were paid a reward of $25,000 by the Iraqi government. PLO members and other terrorists were trained by the Estikhabarat (Iraqi Military Intelligence) at the Salmon Pak facility southeast of Baghdad. Ansar al-Islam, an Al Qaeda affiliate, was also established at a training camp in northeastern Iraq. Saddam provided safe houses in Baghdad for some high-profile terrorists. There is more than just a little evidence that his terror reach went far beyond the Middle East.

The average person is convinced Timothy McVeigh and Terry Nichols were solely responsible for the Oklahoma City bombing that took 168 lives on Apr. 19, 1995. However, neither McVeigh nor Nichols between them had the expertise or the technical skill to carry out such an operation. Hidden Middle Eastern hands are all over the destruction of the Murrah Federal Building.

First of all, the ammonium-nitrate bomb used in the OKC bombing is favored by Middle Eastern terrorist groups. While the formula is not quite "high tech," it would be a hazardous undertaking for a novice. The amount of munition needed to bring down the Murrah Building had to be carefully calculated. The munition, the trigger mechanism, and other bomb components were just not something that could be slapped together by the average Joe from a do-it-yourself manual, as many assert McVeigh and Nichols were able to do. Bomb experts of the highest repute have disputed that either of them could have done so unassisted (Davis, pp. 267, 268). Incidentally, a Ryder truck using the same homemade explosive was used in the first World Trade Center attack on Feb. 26, 1993, an incident perpetrated by men of Middle-Eastern descent.

Secondly, the Ryder truck containing the explosive was spotted at precisely the right part of the building where it would do the maximum amount of damage. Middle Eastern terrorists have known for years that it is neither the blast nor even the flying debris that causes the largest number of deaths in a bomb detonation of this kind, but the collapse of the structure itself. Hence, an examination of photos of terrorist destruction of known Middle Eastern origin will look eerily similar to photos taken of the Murrah Building's destruction.

Thirdly, the Ryder truck had hidden VINs (vehicle identification numbers) removed. This is also part of standard Middle Eastern terrorist operating procedure. A vehicle used in such bombings will often have the VINs removed to prevent authorities from tracing the vehicle back to the perpetrator(s). Whoever altered the truck failed to remove a rear-axle VIN. Whether this was an oversight or done by design to implicate McVeigh and Nichols we cannot say. Nonetheless, it led to McVeigh's capture just two days after the bombing (Apr. 21, 1995). It is very likely the Ryder truck was altered at an auto repair shop near the Murrah Building. This business was owned by another Middle Eastern immigrant (ibid., p. 198-201).

Fourthly, both McVeigh and Nichols were seen by eyewitnesses with Middle Eastern men prior to the terror strike. Edwin Angeles, cofounder of Abu Sayyif, an Islamic-Philippine terror group, witnessed Nichols meeting with Ramzi Yousef in the Philippine town of Cebu City. Yousef was Osama bin Laden's chief bomb maker until his capture in Pakistan on Feb. 14, 1995. Nichols also frequently called a boarding house in Cebu City that was a known hangout of

Islamic militants (ibid. pp. 244, 245). McVeigh was observed by the owner of an Oklahoma City motel in the company of Iraqi "refuges." Among them was a former Iraqi Air Force officer who was seen in the Ryder truck with McVeigh just before the bombing. This man, identified as "John Doe #2," was also seen by eyewitnesses exiting the Ryder truck in the minutes prior to the explosion and leaving the scene in a car driven by McVeigh. All these Iraqis worked for a Palestinian immigrant who was suspected by the FBI of having connections to the PLO (ibid., pp. 1-7).

Saddam Hussein was gradually moving Iraq more and more toward Islamic militancy. In his earlier years he showed not a hint of religiosity. Toward the end of his despotic career he came to embrace the Islamic fundamentalism he once persecuted. He had one of the largest mosques in the Middle East built. He also had a Quran written in his own blood, some-thing only a very dedicated Muslim would do. His ties to jihadist Islam would only have grown tighter were he not removed from power.

Although he was not an *immediate* threat, he represented a permanent and abiding threat to Iraq's religious and ethnic minorities, to the region, and beyond. The mainstream press has beaten the "there-were-no-weapons-of-mass-destruction" drum for so long that many people actually take that statement to be somehow etched in stone on the Holy Mount. However, the Saddam Hussein regime was actively acquiring and developing WMDs and other strategic weapons system in violation of the ceasefire that ended the Gulf War in 1991.

Three years after Iraq was supposed to have terminated its nuclear-weapons program, two thousand scientists and engineers and thousands of technicians were working 24 hours every day to develop a nuclear weapon. At least one device was actually assembled. All it required was a complete nuclear core. There was to be no test detonation. With the complete insanity characterizing this man, Saddam planned to drop it unannounced on Israel (Hamza, pp. 333, 334).

Saddam was apparently still actively involved in trying to obtain fissile material right up until just before Gulf War II. Ambassador Joe Wilson denied that the Iraqi dictator was trying to purchase "yellow cake" (i.e., uranium oxide ore) from the African nation of Niger. Yet, the intelligence services of Britain and other nations confirm this. Just days before American tanks rolled across the Iraqi border from Kuwait, Saddam's regime was attempting to acquire forbidden ballistic missiles from North Korea. Coalition forces have found chemical weapons caches and mobile labs capable of making anthrax and other biological agents. That Saddam had every intention of getting back into the WMD business has been revealed by Project Harmony. There are massive complexes in Iraq yet to be explored for WMD caches, and the CIA seems little interested in investigating them, according to Kenneth Timmerman in his recent book, Shadow Warriors.

America's first modern encounter with jihadist Islam came about as a result of the revolution that brought Ayatollah Rouhollah Khomeini to power in Iran on Feb. 1, 1977. Khomeini demanded the return of the exiled Shah Muhammed Reza Pahlavi. When the United States refused, Iranian students entered the U.S. embassy in Tehran and took 52 hostages. They were held for 444 days. This incident and President Carter's perceived inability to deal with it undoubtedly led to the election of Ronald Reagan in 1980.

Under Khomeini and his successors, Iran has become the chief sponsor of international terrorism. In fact, the Iranian Revolution signaled both a new rise in Islamic militancy and a concomitant rise in terrorism. Iran's support of terrorism is both cynical and Machiavellian. Iran supplies weapons to both the Shiite militias in Iraq and the Sunni insurgents, who then use these weapons to kill each other. We will begin to understand the method to this madness in coming paragraphs.

The Sudan at one time provided assistance and sanctuary to the worst of jihadist bad actors, including Osama bin Laden. In a effort to improve its relations with the United States, the Sudanese government even offered to deliver up bin Laden back in 1998. The Clinton administration refused the offer and the rest, as they say, is history. Since then Sudan has seen fit to terrorize only its own citizens in the southern part of the country.

III. Fourth Generation Warfare and Jihadist Islam

"Fourth generation" warfare was envisioned by William S. Lind and other military thinkers as the type of conflict that would characterize the 21st century. The four generations of warfare are as follows:

First Generation Warfare: Napoleonic battle tactics based on massed artillery at a critical point of the enemy's infantry line followed by overwhelming infantry attack en masse. This system was to be supported by the entire nation's economy and citizenry. Clausewitz termed this type of warfare "total war" in contrast to the limited warfare conducted by the European Grand Monarchies in the previous era. These tactics culminated in mass bloodletting and stalemated trench warfare during World War I. The development of armored vehicles and combat aircraft introduced mechanized warfare toward the end of the war.

Second Generation Warfare: War of mobility based on the tank, mechanized infantry, and aircraft (especially the dive bomber). These ideas were first advocated by H. Liddell Hart and other British army officers. Guderian and other German generals perfected the technique they termed "blitzkrieg." The English Channel halted the blitzkrieg in the West and in the East the Russian winter and the sheer vastness of the country proved too much for the technique, at least as it was practiced by the Germans.

Third Generation Warfare: Nuclear weapons made the overwhelming conventional forces of the Eastern bloc superfluous. Consequently, the communists began to use guerrilla warfare as a means of grand-strategically out flanking the West. Chinese leader Lin Piao called it "encircling the cities of the world," i.e., using national liberation guerrilla movements to deny the West essential Third World raw materials and the exploited cheap labor upon which these extracted raw materials depend.

Fourth Generation Warfare: Also known as "asymmetrical" or "low-intensity" warfare. This kind of warfare is characterized by terrorism and the response of civilized nations to it. Islamic jihadists everywhere have adopted the tactics of terrorism. As an instrument terrorism has really become an end in itself. Terrorism creates social and political chaos. Areas of instability then become safe havens for jihadist groups. These "jihadistans" can then be turned into staging areas for further terrorist operations. We will explain this more fully in a moment. In this type of warfare the line between criminal and political activity has become almost completely erased, since jihadists often finance their terror operations by narcotics trafficking, smuggling, piracy, extortion, etc. Terrorist groups also frequently make ad hoc alliances with criminal syndicates or even hire them out to do some of their dirty work. We could say fourth generation warfare is fedayeen activity of a far more dangerous nature that has gone global.

The last sentence in the previous paragraph is exemplified in Mustafa Nasar's book <u>The Call for a Global Islamic Resistance</u>, a 1600-page pseudo-academic jihadist tome. The dispersion and autonomy of terrorist cells Nasar's book advocates has already inspired bombings in Madrid, London, and Bombay (Cozzen, May 2, 2006). However, it is hard to see how terrorist activity absent even a loose command structure reaching back to a bin Laden or Zarqawi could be fit into an effective overall strategic plan.

Militant Islamic terror groups turn Marx-Leninist guerrilla warfare theory on its head. The communist guerrilla/national liberation movements of the latter half of the 20th cen. would always first create a civilian council composed of loyal members of the communist party or the liberation movement. This group would seek safe haven in another Communist country or in one sympathetic to their cause. They would then recruit idealistic college students and others to train as guerrillas, under experienced mentors who were either veterans of other such wars of liberation, or who were graduates of communist schools of political warfare.

Eventually these cadres would infiltrate into the target country and go through further training in a remote area. They would establish ties to student and other front groups in the capital and other major cities. These groups would raise money, collect necessary equipment, disseminate propaganda, act as spies and couriers, organize demonstrations, and eventually engage in assassination and acts of terror.

When the guerrilla movement was properly trained and equipped in-country and ties to the aforementioned groups established, low-level military operations would begin. These operations would be conducted, at first, by squad and platoon-sized units. Eventually, as sympathy for the movement grew and more recruits began to pour in, larger units would be created and the local people in the countryside would be formed into part-time militia units. The goal was the establishment of a regular army and the creation of a "parallel hierarchy" (i.e., a rival government).

Unlike the jihadists, any terrorism conducted in the above scenario would have a specific purpose, i.e., to eliminate agents or supporters of the central government or to intimidate and strike fear in anyone who might contemplate betraying the movement. These jihadists seem to lack any "party" discipline in their use of terror. It looks more and more like an indiscriminate exercise of violence. In this sense, jihadist terror hasn't even reached any stage described in the literature dealing with guerrilla warfare.

Thus, jihadists operate more like disjointed criminal gangs whose only hope is to create complete chaos so that faith in an established government is completely eroded. They may ensconce themselves in tribal areas where the writ of the established government is already weak. They may make alliances with the local tribes with bribes of money and promises of protection against government agents or rivals. Rival thugocratic jihadistans will be set up in various parts of the country where all governmental authority has broken down. These jihadist gangs may cooperate to bring down the established government. If these rival gangs cannot unify to form a radical Islamic government, they will fight it out until one is top dog.

This seems like an "anti" strategy rather than a legitimate one. However, it has a mad kind of logic to it. It worked to bring in the Taliban regime in Afghanistan from 1995 until it was toppled by a coalition of Western powers and the Northern Alliance in 2001. It also appeared to work, at least for a season, in Somalia, where a Taliban-like government with ties to Al Qaeda was installed in the city of Mogadishu, until the Ethiopian Army, anti-Jihadist Somali militiamen, and U.S. Special Forces recently drove them out. It also had some success in Lebanon. After years of civil war Hizbollah was given autonomy within the country so that a jihadistan can operate openly almost as a state-within-a-state. The jihadists have high hopes terror and the chaos it generates will be the weapon that will bring Iraq into their tyrannical orbit.

Conclusion

We ought not to despair about radical Islam and its use of terror. Undoubtedly, there will be horrific terror incidents in coming years, perhaps even with weapons of mass destruction. It must also be noted that each of the strategic revolutions just discussed was introduced by a totalitarian and aggressive regime. We can take some comfort in the realization that Bonapartism, Communism, and Fascism were defeated in spite of the strategic vision of these ideologies. There is no reason to believe jihadism will fare any better in the end, the terror weapon they wield so effectively notwithstanding.

Glossary of Terms

Ashab: Companions of Muhammed.

Darwish: Called "dervish" in English. Literally, "a beggar going from house to house" (*dar* is Arabic for "door" or "house"). Term came to be applied to mendicant Muslim holymen and then to members of a Sufi lodge or fraternity.

Dhimmi: Member of a "tolerated" religious group, such as Jews and Christians. At one time in Islamic countries dhimmis were forced to pay a special tax (the *jizya*) and to perform humiliating public rituals that showed their second-class status.

Fatiha: The first sura of the Quran.

Fatwa: Religiously based legal judgment on matters of daily Islamic life issued by a *mufti*.

Fedayeen: Literally "self-sacrifice." Arab guerrillas who operated against Israel during the 1940s and 50s. Their attacks were mainly directed against civilian targets. They represent the beginnings of what would become the militant Islamic terrorist movements of today.

Fiqh: Islamic jurisprudence

Five Pillars of Islam: (1) the *shahada*, or the recitation of the formula, "There is no god but Allah, and Muhammed is his prophet," (2) *salat*, the five daily prayers, (3) *zakat*, the giving of alms, (4) *sawn*, the keeping of the sunrise to sunset fast during the month of Ramadan, and (5) the *hajj*, making a pilgrimage to Mecca at least once in a lifetime.

Hadith: "The Tradition," i.e., the record of what Muhammed said, did, allowed (*halal*), or forbade (*haram*).

Hafiz: "Protector." Title given to one who has memorized the entire Quran.

Hajj: A pilgrimage to Mecca that all Muslims are required to perform at least once in a lifetime, if physically or financially possible. One of the Five Pillars of Islam.

Hegira or *Hijra*: Taking place on September 24, 622 A.D. when Muhammed fled from Mecca and took refuge in the city of Yathrib (Medina). However, the actual date was not adopted as the first day of the new era but New Year's Day of the year in which it occurred, i.e., July 15/16 622 A.D. The year of Muhammed's flight marks the beginning of the Muslim chronology. Thus, this year is 1 A.H. (Anno Hegira, "year of the flight") in the Muslim calendar.

Iblis: Quranic corruption of the Greek word *diobolos* or devil.

Ijma: Consensus of Islamic legal authorities.

138

imamites/tudors 93

Anjil 66

Ismailites 94   *67 jinn intermediaries betwe*

Allah + people

Inkilab: Policy of revolution or "overturning" of society envisioned by Baathists as part of a unified Pan-Arab state.

Isnad: The chain of transmitters of a tradition. Also referred to as *sanad*.   *Izrail 67 angel of death*

Jinn: Class of being intermediate between angels *67* and men. They were created out of fire. There are both good and bad jinn. Commonly referred to in English as *genii*. In <u>The Thousand and One Arabian Nights</u> jinn are depicted as beings of great power, able to supernaturally confer wealth and power on favored recipients. Solomon is said to have received occult knowledge from these beings.

Jihad: "Striving," in a personal sense to become a *78* better Muslim, but primarily, "holy war to spread or defend Islam." Considered by Muhammed to be the second-most important principle of Islam. Often called "the Sixth Pillar" of the faith.

Jihadistan: Geographical area controlled by militant jihadists, which can be used as a safe haven for terrorist operations.

Khalifa: "Successor", "deputy", or "representa-*49* tive" of Muhammed. Called "caliph" in English. Khalifa also refers to the caliphate itself, an Islamic state ruled by a caliph.

Madhhab: School of Islamic jurisprudence. Each *89* school has developed its own interpretations of the Quran and Hadith (all are considered orthodox by Sunnis): (1) the Malaki, (2) the Hanafi, (3) the Shafii, and (4) the Hanbali. The Shafii and Hanbali are the strictest interpreters of

52 jizya forced special tax

Kharijites 92,53 3rd party

the Quran and Hadith. The Malaki School inter-prets Islamic law on the basis of the consensus of the *umma*, or the community of the faithful. The Hanbali School uses the principle of analogy to reach legal conclusions.

Mahdi: The "guided one." An eschatological figure who will restore true Islam and destroy all infidels. Sunnis believe the Mahdi will be Jesus of Nazareth. Shiite Imamites believe the Twelfth Imam, Muhammed al-Mahdi, who disappeared one day in the year 880, to be "the hidden Imam." They believe the Hidden Imam will return during a time of great distress as the Mahdi.

Mirab: Niche or recess in a mosque or private home of a Muslim which indicates the *qiblah*.

Mufti: Islamic legal authority or canon lawyer.

Mushrik: One who commits the sin of *shirk*, or associating anything or anyone with Allah. An idolater.

Qiblah: The direction Muslims face while in prayer. The qiblah is always toward Mecca.

Quran: Also known as the Koran. According to Muslims, the complete and final word issued by Allah transmitted to Muhammed by the angel Gabriel over a period of 23 years.

Sahabi: Person who lived in the society of Muhammed.

Salat: The five daily prayers performed by Muslims at prescribed times. One of the Five Pillars of the faith.

Sawn: The keeping of the sunrise to sunset fast during the holy month of Ramadan. A Pillar of Islam.

sabaism lunar worship 80

Sunni 92   Shiites 93   "Twelfers" 93

Shahada (or Kalima): The recitation of the formula, "There is no god but Allah, and Muhammed is his prophet." One of the Five Pillars of Islam.

Sharia: Islamic canon law based on the Quran, Hadith, Ijma, and Qiyas. Legal opinions called *fatwas*, issued by an Islamic legal authority known as a mufti, are also sources for sharia.

Shiites sectarian

Shaytan: Arabic form of "Satan."

Shirk: The unforgiveable sin of "associating" anyone or anything with Allah. *86 Sunni orthodox*

Sunna: An individual example or command given by Muhammed. In this sense *sunna* means "rule" or "statute." *Sunni orthodox Shiite sectarian 86*

Tabiu al-tabiin: Second generation after Muhammed.

Tabiun: The generation that immediately followed Muhammed.

Tekke (or Zawiyah): A Sufi monastery, which has become the center of public worship, often taking the place of the mosque. *Trinity not in Islam 65*

Ulama: Islamic religious authorities.

Umara: Political authority in an Islamic state with the power to enforce the writ of the *ulama*, the religious authority, according to the tenants of Wahhabism.

Umma: Community of the Muslim faithful.

Zakat: The giving of alms. A Pillar of Islam.

93 Torah - law of Moses 67

Wahabism 95   Sufism 95

Saudi Arabia 95

723 Battle of Tours Charles Martel won

References

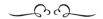

<u>Abingdon Dictionary of Living Religions</u>; "Ahmadiyya"; Abingdon; Nashville, TN; 1981.

Bohannan, Paul & Curtain, Philip; <u>Africa and Africans</u>; The Natural History Press; Garden City, NJ; 1971.

Cole, Donald P.; <u>Nomads of the Nomads</u> The Al Murrah Bedouin of the Empty Quarter; Harlan Davidson, Inc.; Arlington Heights, IL; 1975.

Creasy, E. S.; <u>The Fifteen Decisive Battles of the World</u>; A. F. Burt; NYC, NY; c.1851.

Davis, Jayna; <u>The Third Terrorist</u> The Middle East Connection to the Oklahoma City Bombing; WND Books; Nashville, TN; 2004.

Davis, John, D. (revised by H. S. Gehman); <u>The Westminster Dictionary of the Bible</u>; The Westminster Press; Philadelphia, PA; 1944.

Dundes, Alan (ed.); <u>The Study of Folklore</u>; Prentice Hall, Inc.; Englewood Cliffs, NJ; 1965.

Encyclopedia of Religion; "Druze"; Thompson Gale; Farmington Hills, MI; 2005.

Frankfort, H. and H. A., Wilson, John A., Jacobsen, Thorkild; Before Philosophy (An Essay on Speculative Thought in the Ancient Near East); Penguin Books; Baltimore, MD; 1958.

Gibbon, Edward; The World's Great Events (Vol II); "The Conquest of Persia"; "Arab Conquest of Spain"; P. F. Collier & Son; NYC, NY; 1950.

Cozzens, Jeffrey; "On the arrest of Mustafa bin Abd al-Qadir Setmariam Nasar"; http://www.counterterrorismblog.org/2006/05/on_the_arrest_of_mustafa_bin_a.php; May 2, 2006.

Guillaume, Alfred; Islam; Penguin Books; NYC, NY; 1979.

Gibb, H. A. R. and Kramers, J. H.; Shorter Encyclopedia of Islam; E. J. Brill; Leiden, Netherlands; 1953.

Hallet, Robin; Africa to 1875 A Modern History; University of Michigan Press; Ann Arbor, MI; 1970.

Hamza, K.; Saddam's Bombmaker; Touchstone; NYC, NY; 2000.

Hansen, Eric; Motoring With Mohammed Journeys to Yemen and the Red Sea; Houghton Miller Co.; Boston, MA; 1991.

Henriques, Robert; One Hundred Hours to Suez; The Viking Press, Inc.; NYC, NY; 1957.

Huntington, Samuel P.; The Clash of Civilizations and The Remaking of World Order; Touchstone; NYC, NY; 1996.

Lamsa, George, M.; New Testament Commentary from the Aramaic and the Ancient Customs; A. J. Holman Co.; Philadelphia, PA; 1945.

Langewiesche, William; Sahara Unveiled; Vintage Books; NYC, NY; 1996.

Lawson, Don; Libya and Qaddafi; Franklin Watts; NYC, NY; 1987.

McDowell, Josh; Answers to Tough Questions; Here's Life Publishers, Inc.; San Bernardino, CA; 1980.

Meir-Levi, David; Big Lies: Demolishing the Myths of the Propaganda War Against Israel; Center for the Study of Popular Culture; Los Angeles, CA; 2005.

Morey, Robert A.; Jihad According to the Qur'an and the Hadith; Faith Defenders; Orange, CA; c.1992.

Morey, Robert A.; The Moon-god Allah In the Archaeology of the Middle East; Faith Defenders; Orange, CA; 1994.

Newby, Gordon D.; A Concise Encyclopedia of Islam; Bell & Bain Ltd; Glascow, UK; 2002.

New Catholic Encyclopedia (2nd ed.), Vol.10; "Ottoman Turks"; Thomson Gale; 2003.

Newlon, Clarke; The Middle East — and Why; Dodd, Mead & Co.; NYC, NY; 1977.

Nigosian, S. A.; World Faiths; St. Martin's Press; NYC, NY; 1994.

Palmer, Edward H.; The World's Great Events (Vol. II), "The Hegira"; P. F. Collier & Son; NYC, NY; 1950.

Perrett, Bryan; The Battle Book; Brockhampton Press; London, UK; 1992

Qualben, Lars, P.; A History of the Christian Church; Thomas Nelson & Sons; NYC, NY; 1942.

Samuel, Rinna; Israel and the Holy Land; Golden Press; NYC, NY; 1967.

Shorrosh, Anis A.; Islam Revealed; Thomas Nelson Publishers; Nashville, TN; 1988.

Smith, Huston; The Religions of Man; Harper & Row; NYC, NY; 1958.

Smith, William; Smith's Bible Dictionary; Fleming H. Revell Co.; Old Tappan, NJ; 1984.

Spence, H. D. M. (ed.); The Pulpit Commentary (Vol. 46), "Galatians"; Funk & Wagnalls Co.; NY and London; c.1879.

Spencer, William; The Islamic States in Conflict; Franklin Watts; NYC, NY; 1983.

Strobel, Lee; The Case for Christ; Zondervan Publishing House; Grand Rapids, MI; 1998.

Suskind, Edward; The Sword of the Prophet; Grosset & Dunlap; NYC, NY; 1972.

LaVergne, TN USA
07 November 2010
203868LV00001B/75/P